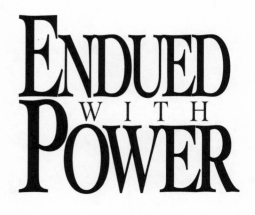

ENDUED WITH POWER

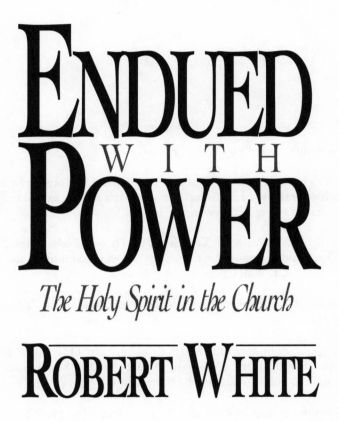

ENDUED WITH POWER

The Holy Spirit in the Church

ROBERT WHITE

A Division of Thomas Nelson Publishers
NASHVILLE

Published in Nashville, Tennessee, by Thomas Nelson, Inc., Publishers, and distributed in Canada by Word Communications, Ltd., Richmond, British Columbia.

Originally published by Pathway Press, Cleveland, Tennessee 37311

Scripture quotations marked *NKJV* are from THE NEW KING JAMES VERSION. Copyright © 1979, 1980, 1982, Thomas Nelson, Inc., Publishers. Used by permission.

Scripture quotations marked *NIV* are from the HOLY BIBLE, NEW INTERNATIONAL VERSION ®. Copyright © 1973, 1978, 1984 by International Bible Society. Used by permission of Zondervan Publishing House. All rights reserved.

Scripture quotations marked *NASB* are from the New American Standard Bible. Copyright © The Lockman foundation 1960, 1962, 1963, 1968, 1971, 1972, 1973, 1975, 1977, 1988. Used by permission.

ISBN 0-7852-7503-7

Printed in the United States of America
1 2 3 4 5 6 — 00 99 98 97 96 95

I dedicate this book to the memory of my grandmother, Viola Graham, and to my mother, Minnie White, who both experienced the Holy Spirit baptism and whose lives and examples provided the environment for me to have a hunger for this experience.

To my family—my wife, Kathryn Shires White, who was reared in the Pentecostal faith, the daughter of the Reverend and Mrs. W.L. Shires, a Church of God minister; my son, Vardaman, who both has received the Holy Spirit baptism and is a minister who proclaims this experience; my daughter, Dr. Alisa W. Coleman, who both enjoys the experience and is a faithful member of the Church of God in Georgia.

This book is especially dedicated to my three grandchildren, Robert Vardaman (Bobby) White, age 9, and Christopher Charles White, age 7, both who have experienced the new birth, and John Michael Coleman, age 7 months. I pray that they will always walk in the light of the full gospel and that they will be filled with the Holy Spirit and used in the Lord's service.

Finally, the book is dedicated to three mentors who had a great impact on my life and ministry: the Reverend W.E. Rodgers, a church planter who communicated to me a burden for planting churches; the Reverend W. Frank Ainsworth who taught me to love the study of God's Word; and the Reverend G.M. Gilbert, a great preacher who taught me a love for preaching.

CONTENTS

FOREWORD

The contemporary Christian world has been dramatically challenged and irreversibly changed by the revival of Pentecost that has swept the world in these last days. The outpouring of the Holy Spirit has transcended geographical and cultural boundaries and is uniting Christians around this planet for world evangelization and the discipling of the nations.

Dr. Robert White, general overseer of the Church of God, Cleveland, Tennessee, America's oldest Pentecostal church, has heeded the call of the Spirit to give to the modern Christian world a contemporary book on the work of the Holy Spirit in the church. *Endued With Power* is a book that addresses this marvelous gift of God to the body of Christ with candor and spiritually intelligent scholarship. One can readily understand from this work that what happened in a small upstairs room in Jerusalem on the church's first Pentecost was just the beginning of God's mighty dealing with men in the church His Son came to build.

Dr. White is himself a wonderful example of the power of the Holy Spirit at work in a man's life. From his humble beginnings in the rural South, he has served the church as a powerful evangelist, a productive pastor, denominational state leader, director of education, World Missions superintendent, seminary president, and now the general overseer of the Church of God, which is represented in more than 130 countries of the world with approximately 4 million members. His voice and wisdom is highly respected in Christianity and Pentecostal circles.

This book is further enhanced by the contribution of some of the finest scholars and writers in the Pentecostal Movement. The total truth of the experience of Holy Spirit baptism and the work of the Holy Spirit in the church is so wonderfully related to the reader that this book is destined to become a classic.

I commend this book to Christians everywhere. Those who have experienced the infilling of Pentecostal power will appreciate the treatment of Pentecostal heritage and purpose. To those who are searching for truth, this book will help them find that there is a Comforter who has come who will teach them all things.

David M. Griffis
Assistant General Director
Youth and Christian Education
Church of God
Cleveland, Tennessee

ACKNOWLEDGMENTS

I wish to express my appreciation to R. Hollis Gause for his scholarly critique of the manuscript and the many valuable suggestions he offered, to Charles W. Conn for reviewing the historical section of the manuscript and contributing his unique insights into the history of the Pentecostal Movement, and especially to Tom George for his work as a researcher and for his suggestions and assistance in editing the manuscript.

INTRODUCTION

Why another book about the Holy Spirit?

During the latter half of this century, the Pentecostal Movement has experienced explosive growth throughout the world. Today, more than 400 million Christians profess the baptism in the Holy Spirit with the evidence of speaking in tongues. Some estimates place the number of Spirit-filled people closer to 1 billion.

Though it is difficult to pinpoint the exact number of Spirit-filled believers, one fact is evident. Interest in the Holy Spirit baptism is greater than at any time in church history. The explosive growth of Pentecostalism has led to an intense interest in knowing more about this gift from God.

Satan, who constantly wages spiritual warfare against believers, attempts to exploit this thirst for knowledge in order to prostitute this blessed experience by doctrinal error and heresy. The book, born out of a burden to provide a biblically based handbook that shows the value of experiencing the Holy Spirit baptism, details the physical evidence of being filled with the Spirit, including the initial evidence; outlines the Spirit's work in the church; and explains the operation of spiritual gifts.

Four highly-qualifed theologians—Dr. R. Hollis Gause, Dr. James Bowers, Dr. Steven J. Land, and Dr. Oliver McMahan—made invaluable contributions to the preparation of this book. All are ministers of the gospel who themselves are Spirit-filled, and it is obvious that they are intimately acquainted with the Holy Spirit of whom they write.

The book is not designed to be an answer to those who seek to undermine the reality of Holy Spirit baptism. Instead, it is a handbook for sincere individuals who hunger for the truth about this wonderful experience. And it also is an instructional manual for teaching and preaching the truth of the Pentecostal power God gave to His church.

It is my prayer that this book will lead believers into experiencing the Holy Spirit baptism and that they, having received the gift, will become bold witnesses for the Lord in these last days, going forth to carry the story of Jesus as men and women of God who are *endued with power!*

The Holy Spirit: Your Personal Guide

1

Dr. R. Hollis Gause is professor of New Testament and theology at the Church of God School of Theology in Cleveland, Tennessee.

Dr. Gause served on the faculty of Lee College for 33 years as registrar and dean of students for three years, dean of the Bible College for 15 years, dean of the Division of Religion for four years, and dean of Lee College for three years. From 1975 through 1978 he served as dean and director of the Church of God School of Theology, as academic dean from 1978 through 1980, and as a member of the faculty since 1982.

R. Hollis Gause

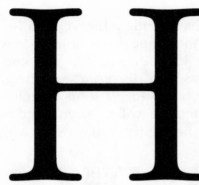ave you ever wished that you could have Jesus physically at your side as He was with the first disciples? Most of us have wished that at one time or another. We imagine that we could ask Him for immediate instruction, or appeal to Him for an immediate answer to prayer, or draw strength from the fact that He is at our side.

Jesus said, however, that His continued physical presence with His disciples would not be good for them (and by application for us): "I tell you the truth; it is expedient [profitable] for you that I go away" (John 16:7). He explained immediately: "If I go not away, the Comforter [Paraclete] will not come unto you; but if I depart, I will send him unto you." At first thought we imagine how wonderful it would be to be always in the physical presence of our Lord. We realize that it is impossible physically for the fleshly body of Jesus to be present with all disciples the world over. Jesus will not be physically among us until the fulfillment of the kingdom of God at His return.

By His physical departure, Jesus has provided for us to have the Holy Spirit, who will give us the benefit of Christ's counsel, wisdom, and guidance. What Jesus was to a small number of disciples by His physical and visible presence the Holy Spirit now is to disciples over the entire world by His spiritual and invisible presence.

It may seem that we have made a broad jump from the word *paraclete* to the name Holy Spirit. If we look at several texts in John 14—16, we will know that this is a term Jesus used in His promise of the gift of the Holy Spirit. In John 14:16, 17 Jesus promised, "I will ask the Father, and He will give you another [Paraclete] that He may be with you forever . . . the Spirit of truth" (*NASB*).

The word *Paraclete* does not appear in most English translations of the Scripture. The King James Version translates it "Comforter" in all places where it appears in John 14—16 (namely, 14:16, 26; 15:26; 16:7). *Paraclete* appears in only one other place in the New Testament, where it is translated "advocate" (1 John 2:1). This text describes Christ as our intercessor in reconciliation.

A related Greek word, *paraklesis*, is used more frequently than *paraclete*. Its meaning and use throw some light on *paraclete*. This word is variously translated in the New Testament as "consolation," "comfort," "exhortation," and "intreaty."

Paraclete can be translated in several ways, depending on how it is used by the writer. The lexicons give the following definitions: one who pleads the cause of another before a judge, counsel for defense, advocate, intercessor, helper, succorer (one who gives relief), aid, defender, and others. It does not mean all these possibilities every time it appears; so we must ask how the word is used to discover its meaning in a particular text in order to determine its meaning in that text.

In this text the answer lies in the expression of Jesus: "another Paraclete"—Comforter. This means that Jesus had been a Paraclete to the disciples and that He would pray the Father to send another who would minister to the disciples in the same way Christ had. Jesus further promised that the coming Paraclete would abide forever (John 14:16). Jesus' function as the first Paraclete tells us what the other Paraclete (the Holy Spirit) would be and do.

Thus we must now ask: What did Jesus do for the disciples while He was among them physically?

The Presence and Ministry of Christ Among the First Disciples

Some issues will be clarified if we observe the things that our Lord did not do for and among His followers. He was not a crutch for their immaturity. On occasion He sent His followers on specific missions (Matthew 10; Luke 10:1-20). For these missions He gave them instructions and ordained them with power appropriate for the message, time, and purpose. When the Seventy wrongly interpreted their power in ministry, Jesus corrected them (Luke 10:17-20). These missions show that Jesus did not encourage a mindless dependency on His physical presence;

instead, He expected them to be interpretive of His instructions about their mission. He did not do everything His disciples wanted Him to do. He remained sovereign over His own actions. His actions were always administrations of grace. He did not yield to the insistence of His disciples to remain in Capernaum. Instead, He fulfilled His Father's commission (Mark 1:35-39). Jesus rebuked James and John for their request for favored positions in the Kingdom (Matthew 20:20-28). He corrected the disciples in their attitude toward children (Matthew 19:13-15). He did not respond to Mary and Martha's concern for Lazarus in the way they expected Him to, nor was He bound by their schedule of action (John 11). Jesus did not always answer his disciples' questions as directly as they asked or expected. Even as late as the Ascension, He did not answer their questions about restoration of the Kingdom as they expected (Acts 1:6-8).

It is more important, however, to observe the positive aspects of Christ's presence among the disciples.

He is the incarnation of God (John 1:14; Matthew 1:23); so, He is the full declaration of God. We see in Him the fullness of grace and truth—the only begotten of the Father (John 1:14). He is "the brightness of his [God's] glory and the express image of his person" (Hebrews 1:3). Jesus is the love and holiness of God fulfilled in His life and death. By His eternal nature and in the fulfillment of His incarnation, He is one with the Father (John 17:21-23). His words are of the Father because the fullness of the Spirit dwells in Him (3:34). For all these reasons, Christ's words "are Spirit, and they are life" (6:63).

Christ's ministry was one of cultivation through teaching, personal example, and redemptive fulfillment. His aim was to bring the disciples to maturity, to prepare them for His physical departure, and to direct them to the Holy Spirit as the Guide who would show them the things of God that they were not able to receive then (John 16:12). It was more important that the disciples be cultivated to this end than it was for Christ to remain with them (v. 7).

The teaching of Christ covers a broad spectrum. It is theological in the formal sense of doctrine. He teaches the ethics of discipleship. He gives instruction and example about prayer. We cannot mention all aspects of His instruction, but we can cite a representative number.

The Sermon on the Mount (Matthew 5—7) covers a wide range of spiritual instruction: spiritual attitudes and affections, witness of being salt and light, spiritual and outward fulfillment of the law, restitution, moral purity, forgiveness of offenders, almsgiving, prayer, trust in God, singleness of mind in discipleship, primacy of the Kingdom, judgment in the Kingdom, fruit bearing, and many other topics. These topics selected out of Matthew 5—7 are repeated in many other contexts in the Gospel records of Christ's life.

In applying these truths, Christ's aim was the spiritual maturity and equipment of the disciples. This involved His correction, rebuke, instruction, and commendation.

He set an example in His own godliness of life. For Himself, He took the law of God seriously and literally. He did not allow violations of the letter on the excuse of the "spiritual intention" of the law. The Word of God was for Him the bread of God. He used it for instruction and for resistance of evil and in conflict with the devil (Matthew 4:1-11; note especially vv. 4, 7, and 10).

He kept His personal relationship with God in clear focus. He came to do His Father's will, even if that meant going to the cross (Luke 22:42-46). This sensitivity directed His ministry. He fulfilled the commission He had from the Father and for which He was anointed by the Holy Spirit (Luke 4:18-21). This set the agenda for a life of obedience not only to the law but also to personal calling. This is exemplary for and instructive to disciples in the fulfillment of their commission.

One of the central issues and practices of Jesus' life was prayer. He prayed through the night. He prayed before significant events—the calling of the Twelve (Luke 6:12-16) and the Crucifixion (Luke 22:42-46). He prayed for others—for the disciples (John 17) and for Peter (Luke 22:31, 32). He fasted and prayed. His ministry included instruction in prayer: the practice of prayer (Matthew 6:5-8), the Lord's Prayer (Matthew 6:9-13; Luke 11:1-4), importunity (persistence) in prayer (Luke 11:5-8), and the relation of prayer to the promises of the Kingdom (Matthew 7:7-11; Luke 11:11-13).

The fulfillment of His life was redemptive. Thus He healed, cast out devils, raised the dead, fed the hungry, and calmed storms.

All these things related to Christ's role in the fulfillment of the last days, which began in the appearances of John the Baptist and Jesus. His presence and ministry fulfilled the kingdom of God for that stage of its development. For this fulfillment He was equipped by the anointing of the Holy Spirit (Luke 4:18-22; John 3:34; Hebrews 1:9). The Kingdom fulfillment culminated in the crucifixion, resurrection, and ascension of Christ. But this was not the final stage of the Kingdom. It must go through a period in which Jesus would be absent physically.

The disciples of the first Christian century and all subsequent centuries had to be prepared for this. We see the results of His physical absence from His disciples for the short time He was in the tomb. They were devastated because they had not seen or believed in the Resurrection, though Jesus had promised it. They did not have the comfort and guidance of the Holy Spirit because Jesus had not yet been glorified (John 7:39). In order to protect them from these effects, our Lord promised the gift of the Holy Spirit—the other Paraclete.

The Presence and Ministry of the Holy Spirit in the Fulfillment of Christ's Promise

It is critical to our understanding of the Holy Spirit's role to emphasize that Jesus promised the Holy Spirit as "another Paraclete." Thus we must understand the nature of Christ's presence and ministry in His first advent as we have summarized above. What Christ did by His physical and local presence the Holy Spirit does in His invisible and universal presence.

From the time of His descent on the Day of Pentecost, the Holy Spirit has been fulfilling the kingdom of God as Christ had done in His earthly ministry. The disciples may have felt that Jesus did not answer their question about the restoration of the Kingdom, but He did. He had promised them the restoration of the Kingdom by the coming of the Holy Spirit (Acts 1:6-8).

Christ is the witness of God as the incarnation of the truth. The Holy Spirit is the witness of God as the Spirit of truth. There is perfect harmony because the Holy Spirit testifies of Christ, and Christ said that His own words are Spirit and life (John 6:63).

Christ is the love of God dwelling among us in the flesh. By the Holy Spirit the love of God has been shed abroad in our hearts (Romans 5:5). Christ is the holiness of God lived out among us. The Holy Spirit is the Spirit of holiness (1:4). He is the divine agent for the fulfilling of the fruit of the Spirit (Galatians 5:22, 23). He is the One in whom we walk in order to fulfill these graces of Christ—the graces of holiness (5:25). He is the Spirit by whom we are born again (John 3:5, 6) and by whom we are sanctified (Romans 15:16; 1 Corinthians 6:11; Hebrews 10:29).

The point of this review is to show the coordination of the ministry of Christ and the ministry of the Holy Spirit. Christ as the Redeemer provided our salvation for us by His perfect life, His atoning death, and His resurrection and ascension into the heavenly Holy of Holies. The Holy Spirit has been sent by Christ from the right hand of God (from the Holy of Holies—the heavenly altar) to fulfill in us all the gifts and promises that Christ has provided as our Redeemer.

Christ fulfilled the kingdom of God by His presence among us—"The kingdom of God is in your midst" (Luke 17:21, *NASB*). The Holy Spirit is the Father's gift of the good things of the Kingdom

(Matthew 7:11; Luke 11:13). After Christ's redemptive mission, the Holy Spirit's coming is the next step in the restoration of the Kingdom (Acts 1:6-8). The coming of the Spirit, the enduement with power, and the witnessing in Jerusalem, Judea, and unto the uttermost parts of the earth constitute the restoration of the kingdom of God. From the Day of Pentecost the church would be acting out the commission of Acts 1:8 and fulfilling the Kingdom under the power of the Holy Spirit. As Christ had directed the activities of the Kingdom while He was on earth (namely, the sending out of the Twelve, Matthew 10; the sending out of the Seventy, Luke 10), the Holy Spirit would direct the activities of the Kingdom in the church. The spread of the witness of Christ is under the direction of the Holy Spirit (Acts 1:8). We see this in operation as the Holy Spirit directed the activities and movements of the early church. The Holy Spirit separated Barnabas and Saul for the work to which He had appointed them (13:1-4). The church laid hands on Barnabas and Saul, but "they, being sent forth by the Holy Ghost, departed unto Seleucia" (v. 4). The Holy Spirit directed the elders and apostles in their judgment that the Gentiles were included in the ministry of grace (15:28). The Holy Spirit directed the ministry of Paul and prohibited him from extending his ministry in Asia (16:6-8). The Holy Spirit directed Paul into Macedonia (16:9, 10).

The sum of these instances of the Spirit's guidance is that Christ exercises the headship of the church and rulership in the Kingdom by the presence and agency of the Holy Spirit.

We have discussed at length the work of the Spirit

in the corporate body. We must understand, however, that what the Spirit is and does in the whole body He is and does in and for the individual members of the body. The union of these two principles appears in 1 Corinthians 3:16, 17 and 6:19, 20. In 3:16, 17 the body of Christ (the church) is the temple of God by the indwelling of the Spirit. In 6:19, 20 individuals in the body are the temple of God by the indwelling of the Spirit. Defilement of the body—whether the corporate body or the individual body—is prohibited in the strongest terms.

In the light of the above, it is appropriate for us to make the corporate activities of the Holy Spirit correspond with activities in the individual believer. Jesus does precisely that in His promise of the Paraclete. John 14—16 contains the elaboration of that promise: The Holy Spirit will abide with us forever (14:16). He is the Spirit of Truth as Christ is the incarnation of truth (14:17; 1:14). The Holy Spirit is with us and shall remain in us (14:17). He will assure us that Christ is with and in the Father (14:20). He will teach us all things and bring all things to our minds (14:26). He will testify of Christ and will give that witness to the disciples (15:26, 27). He will reprove the world of sin, righteousness, and judgment (16:8-11). He will guide us into all truth and show us things to come (16:13). He will bear witness of (i.e., out of/from) the Father and the Son (15:26). He will glorify Christ (16:14). He will show us things of Christ (16:15).

As Christ cultivated the growth and maturity of the disciples while He was in the flesh, the Holy Spirit now cultivates our growth and maturity. This is not intended to imply separation between Jesus and the

Holy Spirit, but unity. In continuing the ministry of Christ, the Holy Spirit fulfills His role as Paraclete, and He is fulfilling the ministry and will of Christ (John 16:12-15).

How does the Holy Spirit do this? There are many ways, but here are a few examples:

He leads us in worship and is the agent of our worship. By the Holy Spirit—the Spirit of adoption—we cry "Abba, Father" (Romans 8:15; Galatians 4:6). He guides us in praying. When we do not know how to pray, He helps our infirmities and makes intercession for us with unutterable groanings (Romans 8:26). He makes intercession for the saints according to the will of God (v. 27).

Paul spoke of praying both with the Spirit and with the understanding as well as singing both with the Spirit and with the understanding (1 Corinthians 14:15).

The early church prayed in the Holy Spirit when it was under threat (Acts 4:23-31). The body was in one mind and prayed with one voice (v. 24). They asked God to stretch forth His hand in signs and wonders in the name of His Son Jesus (v. 30). The place was shaken and the disciples were filled with the Holy Spirit and spoke the word of God with boldness (v. 31). They all believed with one heart and one soul (v. 32). Paul exhorted to pray always "with all prayer and supplication in the Spirit" (Ephesians 6:18), and Jude exhorted to "[build] up yourselves on your most holy faith, praying in the Holy Ghost" (Jude 20).

We are to be filled with the Spirit, and this fullness is manifested in specific spiritual experiences: "speaking to [ourselves] in psalms and hymns and spiritual songs, singing [in the Spirit], making melody in [our] heart to the Lord" (Ephesians 5:18, 19). This Spirit-filled experience also manifests itself in our "giving thanks always for all things" (v. 20) and in our submission one to another (v. 21).

The witness of the Holy Spirit is fundamental to our confession in worship. He gives us witness that we are the children of God, bearing witness with our spirits that we are the children of God (Romans 8:15, 16; Galatians 4:5, 6). The Holy Spirit leads us as the children of God (Romans 8:14). The Holy Spirit gives the testimony that Jesus is Lord (1 Corinthians 12:3).

The Holy Spirit cultivates in us the graces that He implanted in the new birth. He makes us "free from the law of sin and death" (Romans 8:2). By walking in the Spirit, we fulfill the righteousness of the law (v. 4). He gives us a spiritual mind and, with that, life and peace (vv. 5, 6). By giving us the life of the resurrected Lord, the Holy Spirit assures us of the quickening of our mortal bodies in the resurrection (v. 11). It is by the Holy Spirit that we groan in ourselves in anticipation of the resurrection (v. 23). He assures us that suffering is witness of healing and death is evidence of resurrection.

The graces of the new birth are called "the fruit of the Spirit" (Galatians 5:22) and "the fruit of the light" (Ephesians 5:9, *NIV*). These are the graces our Lord taught in His earthly ministry and now teaches us by the Holy Spirit. As the early disciples walked with Jesus in His steps, the Holy Spirit calls us to walk in Him: "Since we live by the Spirit, let us keep in step with the Spirit" (Galatians 5:25, *NIV*).

There are important differences in the transition from Christ's physical presence to the outpouring of the Holy Spirit. This transition is represented in Christ's resurrection appearance recorded in John 20:19-23. In this appearance Jesus showed the disciples the wounds of His crucifixion. By this He established that His identity as crucified Lord is one with His identity as resurrected Lord. As the resurrected Lord, He now gives what He had purchased by the atonement in His crucifixion. This is His legacy of redemption. It consists of His peace ("Peace be unto you," vv. 19, 21); a commission ("As my Father hath sent me, even so send I you," v. 21; cf. Luke 4:18, 19); and the gift of the Holy Spirit ("He breathed on them and said to them, 'Receive the Holy Spirit,'" John 20:22, *NASB*). As Christ had gone out from the Father under a commission of proclamation of the gospel, He was now sending the disciples under the same commission. As Christ had gone out from the Father under the anointing of the Holy Spirit, He was now sending the disciples out under the anointing of the same Spirit. This appearance and legacy prepared the disciples for the outpouring of the Holy Spirit on the Day of Pentecost. And the promise holds from the age of the apostles to the end of this age: "The promise is unto you, and to your children, and to all that are afar off, even as many as the Lord our God shall call" (Acts 2:39).

There are other important differences to be noted. They relate to the nature of Christ and the Holy Spirit and to the transition from the time of Christ's redemptive provision to the time of the Holy Spirit's redemptive fulfillment. Christ as the Word of God is the decree of God. The Holy Spirit carries out the decree of God. Christ's redemptive provision fulfills the old covenant and introduces the new covenant. The Holy Spirit reveals the new covenant (as He had revealed the old), and He becomes the foretaste and seal of the new. Christ continues His ministry in heaven and will culminate it in His return in glory.

The ministry of the Holy Spirit continues and will continue until the fulfillment of the kingdom of God. He is the gift of God for the last days. He continues in this role until the last days shall be fulfilled. Jesus promised, "He that believeth on me, the works that I do shall he do also; and greater works than these shall he do" (John 14:12). This could hardly refer to more spectacular works than our Lord performed. It could be seen as referring to works that are more numerous and more widespread in influence. But it seems more likely that these works of the Holy Spirit in the lives of disciples of Christ will be greater because of their relationship to the fulfillment of the Kingdom. Every sign and wonder that occurs in this age is a renewed announcement of the fulfillment of the kingdom of God. They are announcements of the imminence of Christ's return and reign. These things will continue and will lead into the fulfillment of the Kingdom. In this sense they are greater.

This ministry of the Holy Spirit will continue for as many generations as the Lord tarries until He comes again. To complete His mission, Christ had to die, be raised again, and ascend to the Father. The Holy Spirit does not have to die in order to fulfill His mission, because Christ our Passover has been offered for us (1 Corinthians 5:7) and all provisions of the Atonement stand completed (Hebrews 9:26).

Therefore, the Holy Spirit does not have to be raised from the dead. Christ is our resurrection in the power of the Spirit; therefore, the Spirit will quicken our mortal bodies (Romans 8:11). He bears witness of the age to come until it is fulfilled.

The Holy Spirit does not have to ascend to prepare a place for us. Christ is doing that (John 14:1-4). The Holy Spirit is the foretaste and the guarantee in kind of the place that Christ is preparing for us. He will continue to be God's stamp of authenticity and ownership (signet ring) on the believer until the believer inherits all things that Christ has prepared for God's children.

O boundless love divine, how shall this tongue of mine,
To wond'ring mortals tell the matchless grace divine,
That I, a child of hell, should in His image shine!
The Comforter has come!

The Comforter has come,
The Comforter has come!
The Holy Ghost from heaven,
The Father's promise given;
O spread the tidings 'round,
Wherever man is found,
The Comforter has come!

—William J. Kirkpatrick

Experiencing the Baptism in the Holy Spirit

2

Dr. James P. Bowers is pastor of the Scenic View Church of God in Scottsboro, Alabama.

Dr. Bowers serves as adjunct professor in discipleship and Christian formation at the Church of God School of Theology in Cleveland, Tennessee. Additionally, he is on the seminary's Pastoral Advising Board, a group of pastors who mentor students and advise faculty regarding the needs of local church communities.

CHAPTER 2

James P. Bowers

ontemporary Christians live in a time of increased emphasis on the person and work of the Holy Spirit. Popular religious books, scholarly theological treatises, Christian television, and the changing worship styles of various denominations all reflect a resurgent interest in the significance of the Holy Spirit for believers, the church, and the world. The Holy Spirit is no longer the neglected person of the Trinity, having moved from the periphery to the center stage of Christian concern. To even the most casual observer, it is apparent that the Christian church has entered the age of the Spirit.

Renewal of interest in the Holy Spirit in the larger Christian community follows the birth of the modern Pentecostal Movement. And yet many Christians (and some Charismatics), while generally receptive to the ministry of the Holy Spirit, still do not embrace the original Pentecostal teaching of a separate experience of Spirit baptism after conversion. In the current generic Pentecostal atmosphere in contemporary Christianity, there is also a very real danger that Pentecostals themselves may lose sight of the importance of this distinctive experience. It is vital, therefore, that we understand why we should receive the baptism in the Holy Spirit, what difference it makes in our lives, and how to receive this spiritual experience.

Why Receive the Baptism in the Holy Spirit?

A.J. Tomlinson, the first general overseer of the Church of God, once stated concerning the importance of personal experience in salvation: "And to fully understand these subjects is not so important any way as to have a real and full experience." [1] Tomlinson was expressing a conviction of the early Pentecostal Movement that true Christianity required a heart-deep spiritual experience with God. Unfortunately, even Pentecostals can mistakenly consider their Pentecostal label, charismatic worship style, or belief in the charismatic gifts a substitute for a real and full experience of Pentecost. Nothing less than an *authentic* personal experience of Spirit baptism and a continuing manifestation of its power will result in a Spirit-filled life. Four scripturally based reasons can be identified for receiving the baptism in the Holy Spirit.

The Command of Christ

It should first be noted that the Scriptures clearly present receptivity to baptism in the Holy Spirit as the commandment of Christ to His followers. John the

Baptist's message described the Spirit's outpouring as the personal work of Christ in the lives of the repentant: "I baptize you with water, but he will baptize you with the Holy Spirit" (Mark 1:8). Christ specifically *commanded* His disciples to "wait for the gift my Father promised" (Acts 1:4). Thus, receiving the promised baptism in the Holy Spirit was not a take-it-or-leave-it option for the disciples but the command of Christ. Consequently, it was a matter of faithful discipleship for them, as it is for believers today. We too have the commandment of Christ to "receive the Holy Spirit" (John 20:22).

The Universal Provision

Not only is there a commandment to receive the Holy Spirit, but there is also a universal provision for all believers to do so. This was suggested by Peter's quotation of Joel's prophecy (Acts 2:17-21) in his sermon on the Day of Pentecost: "In the last days, God says, I will pour out my Spirit on all people" (v. 17). The provision was made explicit when Peter later declared, "Repent and be baptized, every one of you, in the name of Jesus Christ for the forgiveness of your sins. And you will receive the gift of the Holy Spirit. The promise is for you and your children and for all who are far off—for all whom the Lord our God will call" (vv. 38, 39).

We then find recorded in Acts several accounts of believers being baptized in the Holy Spirit that confirm the truth of Peter's words (see 4:23-31; 8:9-17; 10:24-28; 19:1-7). Moreover, historical research and the contemporary experience of literally millions of believers show that Spirit baptism continues to be a viable part of Christian life to the present day.[2] God's universal provision for experiencing Spirit baptism tells us that all believers should be receptive to this dimension of relationship with the Holy Spirit.

Communion With the Holy Spirit

Concern for a growing fellowship with the Holy Spirit provides another reason for receiving the baptism. Spirit baptism is, among other things, an experience *in relationship* with the Holy Spirit. Although conversion (regeneration) represents the believer's initial transformation by the Spirit, there is also a *qualitative* change in our relationship with the Holy Spirit in the baptism experience. That change in relationship opens a new realm of spiritual possibilities for the believer—scripturally described as the *Spirit-filled* life.[3] In Spirit baptism, the previously *indwelling* Spirit now *fills* the believer's life. Or, as J. Rodman Williams explained, "The Spirit who is totally present now totally claims the person."[4] This suggests that Spirit baptism is an essential experience in the believer's relationship with the Holy Spirit. Christian discipleship—specifically, communion with the Holy Spirit—is incomplete without an experience of Spirit baptism.

The Church's Mission

Lastly, believers need to receive the baptism in the Holy Spirit to be spiritually equipped for the God-given mission of the church. When Christ's disciples asked about the restoration of the Kingdom and the end of all things, Jesus responded, "It is not for you to know the times or dates the Father has set by his own authority. But you will receive power when the Holy Spirit comes on you; and you will be my witnesses in Jerusalem, and in all Judea and Samaria, and to the ends of the earth" (Acts 1:7, 8).

With those words, Jesus promised His disciples power for service in the baptism with the Holy Spirit. To fulfill their role in the church's mission of proclaiming the gospel and making disciples, they needed to be divinely enabled and strengthened. This empowerment was provided in their baptism with the Holy Spirit on the Day of Pentecost and attested by wonders, signs, and miracles in the life of the church. Believers today continue to need this supernatural endowment of power for service to be effective participants in the church's mission in the world.

To summarize, believers need to receive the baptism in the Holy Spirit for four basic reasons. Obedience to the command of Christ, responsiveness to God's universal provision, continuing growth in fellowship with the Holy Spirit, and the demands of the church's mission make Spirit baptism an essential experience in Christian discipleship. Personal appropriation of the spiritual blessings of the Spirit-filled life can only be a reality when we receive the baptism in the Holy Spirit.

What Difference Does Spirit Baptism Make?

What has been said about the necessity of receiving the baptism with the Holy Spirit suggests the life-changing potential of this experience for believers. Spirit baptism is not a spiritual experience of mere momentary significance. Its influence extends beyond the initial infilling of the Spirit to shape the character of the Christian life. The baptism in the Holy Spirit, therefore, is best understood as "an initiating experience for the believer."⁵ That is, it ushers one into the realm of the spiritual abundance of the Spirit-filled life. The dimensions of this life in the Spirit reveal the difference Spirit baptism makes in the believer.

The Presence of the Spirit

Perhaps the most obvious dimension of the Spirit-filled life manifested in the believer who has received Spirit baptism is a heightened awareness of the presence of the Holy Spirit. Jesus told His disciples that the promised Holy Spirit would be "another Counselor to be with you forever" (John 14:16). This is the reality known by the Spirit-filled believer—a discernible presence and activity of God's Spirit in one's life. Those baptized with the Spirit have a testimony of living in the "conscious presence of God" as the Spirit guides, teaches, and empowers them.⁶ Their lives are characterized by a dynamic relationship with Christ through the Spirit. They know by personal experience, as they make their spiritual journey, that Christ has not left them "orphans" (John 14:18). But rather, they have a "vivid sense of the Spirit's presence and power" in their lives.⁷

Walking in the Spirit

To truly live in the Spirit's presence is to "walk in the Spirit" (Galatians 5:25, KJV). This dimension of the Spirit-filled life calls the believer to the privilege and responsibility of cooperating with a continuing process of spiritual transformation. The danger, even for one baptized in the Spirit, is to stop living by the Spirit and to manifest the works of the flesh.[8] Thus, Paul exhorted the Galatians, "Since we live by the Spirit, let us keep in step with the Spirit" (v. 25). The opportunity, given the enabling presence of the Spirit, is to see the fruit of the Spirit produced in one's life.[9]

Spirit baptism, then, is not the end point of Christian experience. It does represent a definite spiritual transition to a new level of relationship with the Holy Spirit. Conversion accomplishes the initial inward spiritual renewal and establishes fellowship with God. Sanctification continues the redemptive process through spiritual cleansing, which confirms the believer in wholehearted devotion to God manifested in holiness of life. Spirit baptism is the believer's specific spiritual preparation for ministry and provides the essential impetus for cultivation of the fruit, graces, and gifts of the Spirit-filled life.[10]

Within this ongoing process of spiritual renewal, additional fillings of the Spirit are possible and a continuing personal appropriation of God's grace is necessary.[11] The believer must continually, as Paul insisted, "be filled with the Spirit" (Ephesians 5:18). The baptism with the Holy Spirit empowers the believer for this ongoing journey and process of transformation in the Spirit.

Holiness of Heart and Life

Walking in the Spirit leads the believer into another important dimension of the Spirit-filled life—holiness of heart and life. We must remember that the Spirit who fills the believer is "the Spirit of holiness" (Romans 1:4). Holiness describes the nature of the

Spirit and shapes the character of the Spirit-filled believer. Paul reproved the immorality of the Corinthians with a question: "Do you not know that your body is a temple of the Holy Spirit, who is in you, whom you have received from God?" (1 Corinthians 6:19). Clearly, the apostle considered an unholy life incompatible with the presence of the Holy Spirit.

As early Pentecostals believed, this suggests that the baptism with the Holy Spirit has moral (holiness) as well as charismatic (power) effects.[12] Consequently, we can conclude that "holiness of life is the primary manifestation of the Holy Spirit-filled life."[13] At the very least, this tells us that character and charismatic gifts, power and holiness, love and ministry must not be separated. As Paul suggested in 1 Corinthians 12—14, love is the only appropriate motivation for Spirit-directed ministry. The fruit of the Spirit, especially love, is to guide the exercise of the gifts of the Spirit.

Spirit baptism enables the believer for this life of holiness. The power of the Spirit makes possible a life of victory over sin and rejection of the works of the flesh: "One is filled with the Spirit, not fear, lust or greed."[14] The fruit of the Spirit can then flourish in the strength of the Spirit. To be filled with the Spirit is to be empowered for righteous living and holy service by the same Holy Spirit.

Fellowship in the Spirit

The Spirit's work of producing a unity of holiness and power (or holy power) in the Spirit-filled believer anticipates the unity of fellowship believers enjoy in the Spirit. Again, we need to remember that Spirit baptism is not a spiritual experience that affects the believer only when it is received. Rather, it shapes and directs one's subsequent manner of life. In other words, Pentecost did not end with Acts 2:4. And neither should we view the baptism with the Holy Spirit as merely an individual experience. It is interesting, in this regard, to note the corporate context of outpourings of the Spirit in Acts. A significant dimension of life in the Spirit is expressed in the fellowship shared by Spirit-filled believers.

Perhaps this is why Luke described the fellowship of the Spirit-filled community of believers in Acts 2:42-47. There we see the relationships and disciplines of a charismatic community—prayer and worship, teaching, fellowship, ministry to those in need, and witness. Believers participated with each other in these experiences of community life in the power of the Spirit with "many wonders and miraculous signs." A unity of fellowship resulted, and their commitment to unity shaped their polity (church government) and led them to handle differences in ways intended to preserve fellowship.[15] Their Pentecost experience provided the power needed to be a community of reconciliation that, by the unity of their fellowship in the Spirit, looked forward to the time when all things would be reconciled under the lordship of Jesus Christ.

A Missionary Passion and Power

The last dimension of the Spirit-filled life resulting from an experience of the baptism with the Holy Spirit is the missionary passion and power unleashed in the heart and life of the believer. Jesus said to His disciples concerning Spirit baptism, "But you will receive power when the Holy Spirit comes on you; and you will be my witnesses" (Acts 1:8). The baptism in the Holy Spirit imparts a zeal for God's redemptive mission in the world and spiritually commissions the believer into ministry in the power of the Spirit.

With the passionate missionary impulse of the Spirit come also supernatural enablements—power for service—for the ministry efforts of believers. Spiritual gifts and ministries given by the Spirit equip God's people for their mission and spiritually affirm the priesthood of all believers. Apostles, prophets, teachers, miracle workers, gifts of healing, administration, tongues, interpretation, and so on, are given to build up the church and to make possible the realization of its mission (1 Corinthians 12:27-31). The presence and power of the Spirit create a sense of urgency for Kingdom work in light of Christ's soon return. Spirit-filled believers are called of Christ by the Spirit to commit themselves to their missionary vocation and to be willing to be an instrument of the Spirit for the advancement of the kingdom of God.

Receiving the Holy Spirit baptism brings the believer into the fullness of the Spirit's presence and power. The personal presence of the Spirit is a reality as the believer continues to walk in the Spirit. The power of the Spirit is then manifested in holiness, unity of fellowship with other believers, and a passion for mission and ministry. Experiencing the baptism in the Holy Spirit and the continuing dimensions of life in the Spirit enables the believer to be the powerful witness needed for the work of Christ's kingdom.

Receiving the Baptism With the Holy Spirit

Knowing the blessings of the Spirit-filled life depends on an *authentic* experience of Spirit baptism. To personally receive Holy Spirit baptism, the believer must avoid certain mistaken ideas and practices and embrace the very real spiritual conditions for the experience. Contrasting God's generosity with that of earthly fathers, Jesus once exclaimed to His disciples, "How much more will your Father in heaven give the Holy Spirit to those who ask him!" (Luke 11:13). Having the right perspective can help us to ask for the gift of the Spirit in a manner certain to lead to a fulfillment of Christ's promise in our lives.

Perspective

The proper perspective on receiving the Baptism begins with the reminder that all we receive from God comes by grace through faith. Nothing we can do earns or merits any of God's blessings. This is especially true concerning Spirit baptism. The rebuke of Simon the sorcerer in the face of his attempt to acquire the gift of God with money reflects this truth (Acts 8:9-25). Of course, most believers would never attempt such a thing, but they may find themselves with a misguided perspective that expects certain personal sacrifices or religious acts to earn the right to receive the gift of the Spirit. Such a perspective will only hinder realization of the Spirit-filled life. We cannot earn what is a gift of God. We simply need to be spiritually ready to receive.

Spiritual readiness for receiving Spirit baptism is a matter of relationship with God. To desire the fullness of the Spirit is not to seek spiritual manifestations such as tongues.[16] Rather, it is to pursue a deeper relationship with God. Therefore, the conditions for this experience are descriptions of "relationships that are important to spirituality and the blessing of the Holy Spirit."[17] Nothing can be added to faith, but faith manifests itself in spiritual relationships. Thus, certain relationships are expressions of faith and are essential to receiving baptism in the Holy Spirit.[18]

Relationships

The initial relational condition for receiving the baptism with the Holy Spirit is that one is a believer in Jesus Christ. On the Day of Pentecost, it was believers who were "filled with the Holy Spirit and began to speak in other tongues" (Acts 2:4). Peter's Pentecost sermon extended the promise of the gift of the Holy Spirit to those who would repent, be baptized, and receive forgiveness of sins in the name of Jesus Christ (vv. 38, 39). In Samaria those receiving the Spirit had previously accepted the word of God, and those in Ephesus were disciples before being filled with the Spirit (8:9-25; 19:1-7). Although there are occasions when individuals experience salvation and the infilling of the Spirit almost simultaneously, even then a relationship of saving faith in Christ spiritually precedes receiving baptism in the Holy Spirit.

Commitment to discipleship is another spiritual-relational condition for receiving the Spirit. This relationship is suggested in the Book of Acts by the giving of the Spirit to those who were identified as disciples of Christ. Their discipleship was confirmed by their obedience of Christ's command to wait for the gift the Father had promised and their acceptance of Christ's charge to be His witnesses (1:4, 8).

Early in this century, Pentecostals understood their experience of Spirit baptism as yet another of the "waymarks" in their Christian discipleship.[19] Such things as faith, humility, submissiveness to God, and purity and holiness characterized the discipleship of those seeking to know the fullness of the Spirit. Preparation for baptism in the Holy Spirit still requires such a relationship of obedient discipleship.

Lastly, sanctification is an essential condition for baptism in the Holy Spirit. As noted earlier, the Holy Spirit who fills the believer is "the Spirit of holiness" (Romans 1:4). Sanctification has to do with relationship—relationship to God, others, self, and world. Thus, John Wesley taught that sanctification was perfection in love—to love God supremely and your neighbor as yourself.[20] To be filled with the Spirit of God, we must be cleansed of all love for sin, the flesh, and the world. Realization of this fact led early Pentecostal believers to the conviction that "the Holy Ghost will not dwell in an unclean temple."[21] If one is to be prepared for an authentic experience of the Spirit's fullness, there must be a purging of desires and affections that would resist the reign of the Spirit in one's life.

Practical Considerations

Once attention has been given to the necessary spiritual relationships, other practical considerations can be helpful for the person desiring to receive the baptism in the Holy Spirit. These considerations are suggested by scriptural and theological perspectives on the experience of Spirit baptism. They offer guidance about how the baptism with the Holy Spirit can be personally received when the believer is otherwise spiritually prepared.

Faith. The person desiring to receive baptism in the Holy Spirit must trust God to fulfill His promise to give the gift of the Spirit. This kind of faith, however, does not claim prematurely to have received what has not been personally experienced. There are those who mistakenly teach believers to claim the baptism with the Holy Spirit whether there is any sign of the experience or not. This is not faith but presumption. Christ did not tell His disciples to claim the gift; but rather, acting on their faith, they were to "wait for the gift" (Acts 1:4). An *authentic* experience of Spirit baptism will result only when our faith (trusting God to fill us) finds fulfillment in what God has, in fact, accomplished in us.[22]

Prayer. Faith that Christ would send the promised gift of the Spirit led the early disciples to join "together constantly in prayer" (Acts 1:14). Prayer was also especially prominent in the accounts of believers receiving the baptism with the Holy Spirit (2:1; 4:31; 8:15). This should not be taken to mean, however, that prayer—especially some mechanical prayer formula or repetitive phrases—is the scriptural way to experience Spirit baptism. Rather, "prayer is more properly the spiritual environment in which the Spirit is often bestowed."[23] Prayer can help deepen our communion with God and make us more receptive to the gift of the Spirit. It can prove beneficial for those desiring the Spirit's fullness to give themselves to prayer, especially in a fellowship of prayer with other believers.

Worship. Whatever our mode of seeking God, the

fundamental concern is the worship of God. In the various circumstances of the Spirit's outpouring in Acts—prayer, praise, hearing the gospel preached—the common denominator was the worship of God.[24] This must undoubtedly explain the testimonies of those today who experience the infilling of the Holy Spirit during times of corporate worship of God without necessarily seeking the experience. This tells us that God should be the focus of those desiring the fullness of God's Spirit. "In all of our seeking we must place greater affection on the Giver of the experience than upon the experience."[25]

Yielding to the Spirit. Even with God as the focus of faith, prayer, and worship, there yet remains a need for a personal willingness to receive the Spirit. In this regard, Roger Stronstad has commented on the use of the phrases "filled with the Holy Spirit" and "received the Holy Spirit" in Acts. He notes that God always *fills* with the Spirit, but only when believers *actively receive* the Spirit. There is a complementary relationship between being filled and receiving the Spirit. Both are necessary.[26] Consequently, the believer who would experience the baptism in the Holy Spirit must be actively receptive to this spiritual blessing. God has the initiative in bestowing the gift, but He never imposes it on those who have no hunger for the Spirit's fullness. Experiencing baptism in the Spirit becomes a reality in our lives when we yield ourselves to the Spirit's sovereign presence and power.

The last-days outpouring of the Spirit in our time is reshaping and empowering the lives of believers around the world. With nearly a century of

Pentecostal renewal behind us, the question at the heart of the movement is the same one Paul asked the Ephesian disciples: "Did you receive the Holy Spirit when you believed?" (Acts 19:2). Nothing less than a personal experience of the baptism with the Holy Spirit will bring us the gift of the Spirit-filled life Christ promised us.

*Scripture references in this chapter are from the *New International Version.*

Endnotes

[1] Homer A. Tomlinson, ed., *Diary of A.J. Tomlinson, Volume One*, 1901-1923 (New York: Ryder Press, 1949), p. 133.

[2] For historical perspectives, see Wade H. Horton, ed., *The Glossolalia Phenomenon* (Cleveland, Tenn.: Pathway Press, 1966) and Ronald A.N. Kydd, *Charismatic Gifts in the Early Church* (Peabody, Mass.: Hendrickson Publishers, Inc., 1984).

[3] The dimensions of the Spirit-filled life are outlined in this chapter. Such a lifestyle involves a continuing fellowship with the Holy Spirit and manifestation of the fruit, graces, and gifts of the Spirit. Since the baptism in the Holy Spirit brings the believer into the Spirit-filled life, it is proper to emphasize the qualitative change in relationship with the Spirit represented by the experience.

[4] J. Rodman Williams, "Baptism in the Holy Spirit," *Dictionary of Pentecostal and Charismatic Movements*, eds. Stanley M. Burgess and Gary B.

McGee (Grand Rapids: Zondervan Publishing House, 1988), pp. 40-48.

[5]R. Hollis Gause, *Living in the Spirit: The Way of Salvation* (Cleveland, Tenn.: Pathway Press, 1980), p. 63.

[6]Julia McCallie Divine, "My Inheritance," *Evangel,* May 1, 1910, pp. 5, 6.

[7]Williams, p. 41.

[8]Paul identified the works of the flesh as "sexual immorality, impurity and debauchery; idolatry and witchcraft; hatred, discord, jealousy, fits of rage, selfish ambition, dissensions, factions and envy; drunkenness, orgies and the like" (Galatians 5:19-21). He was clear that those who "live by the Spirit" can and should avoid such things.

[9]The fruit of the Spirit is "love, joy, peace, patience, kindness, goodness, faithfulness, gentleness and self-control" (Galatians 5:22, 23). Steve Land noted, "The fruit of the Spirit is one because the Spirit is the sole source and the fruit is the character of God." See Steven J. Land, *Pentecostal Spirituality: A Passion for the Kingdom* (Sheffield, England: Sheffield Academic Press, 1993), p. 205.

[10]Gause, p. 98; James P. Bowers, "A Wesleyan-Pentecostal Vision of the Christian Life With Pedagogical Implications for Christian Education" (E.D. dissertation, Southern Baptist Theological Seminary, 1990), pp. 151-156.

[11]Acts 4:23-31 describes another outpouring of the Spirit on believers who had previously been filled. French Arrington comments, "This was a renewed fill-

ing of the Spirit" in *The Acts of the Apostles: An Introduction and Commentary* (Peabody, Mass.: Hendrickson Publishers, 1988), p. 50. As circumstances warrant, believers may experience additional fillings or equippings of the Spirit after their initial baptism in the Holy Spirit.

[12]Bowers, pp. 155, 156, and Gause, pp. 95–104.

[13]Gause, p. 72.

[14]Land, p. 203.

[15]This concern was expressed in the Jerusalem Council's practice of Spirit-led consensus in their decision making. The explanation given for their conclusions was "It seemed good to the Holy Spirit and to us . . ." (Acts 15:28). Early Pentecostals operated with a similar approach (Bowers, p. 183).

[16]See Gause's excellent discussion of various "pitfalls" to be avoided in seeking for the fullness of the Spirit (*Living in the Spirit*, pp. 73-75).

[17]*Ibid.*, p. 73.

[18]Williams, p. 48.

[19]*Minutes of the Twenty-Second Annual Assembly of the Churches of God* (Cleveland, Tenn.: Church of God Publishing House, 1927), p. 8.

[20]Harold Lindstrom, *Wesley and Sanctification* (Wilmore, Ky.: Francis Asbury Publishing Company, 1980), p. 136; W.E. Sangster, *The Path to Perfection* (New York: Abingdon-Cokesbury, 1943), p. 155.

[21]Bowers, p. 151.

[22]Roger Stronstad, *The Charismatic Theology of St. Luke* (Peabody, Mass.: Hendrickson Publishers, Inc., 1984), p. 81.

[23] *Ibid,* p. 70.

[24] Gause, p. 85.

[25] *Ibid.*

[26] Stronstad, p. 71.

The Nature and Evidence of Spiritual Fullness

3

Dr. Steven J. Land is academic dean and associate professor of Pentecostal theology at the Church of God School of Theology in Cleveland, Tennessee.

Dr. Land is an ordained minister in the Church of God with 23 years of pastoral experience. He has been on the faculty of the School of Theology since 1979.

CHAPTER 3

Steven J. Land

Jesus commanded the early Christians to tarry in Jerusalem until they were filled with the Spirit (Acts 1:4-8). Paul instructed the church at Ephesus to keep on being filled with the Spirit (Ephesians 5:18). But how does one go about proving one is filled with the Spirit? From the beginning, observers apparently could conclude that Spirit-filled believers appeared to be drunk (Acts 2:13, 15; Ephesians 5:18) or to be speaking unintelligible gibberish and behaving in an unfamiliar and unsettling way. In the 2,000 years since the incarnation of our Savior, various evidences have been adduced for being filled with the Spirit. How should a Christian go about deciding which evidence is false, which is true, and of the true that which is fundamental or normative? To prove something is to demonstrate its validity and genuineness. How and under what circumstances does speaking in tongues count as evidence of being filled with the Spirit? From the beginning, Pentecostals were accused of being deranged or demonized. How should Pentecostals make their case before the public and among other Christians? In this chapter we will consider the age in which we live, the problem of conflicting evidence, and the nature of spiritual evidence. In this way we will focus on the initial, essential, and ultimate evidence of Holy Spirit baptism.

The Age in Which We Live

We live in a scientific, hedonistic, and violent age. A scientific age seeks to publicly demonstrate by the scientific method the truth or validity of various claims. Since the Enlightenment of the 18th century, scientific knowledge has consisted of publicly demonstrable facts which purportedly describe reality. Though scientific theories come and go, science has achieved a remarkable degree of technical proficiency. Because of Christianity the world was viewed as behaving lawfully and therefore science was possible.

In addition to the evidence of the five senses, however, Christians have always maintained that there is revelation from God. God enables us to hear His voice, to see His mighty hand at work around us, and to know Him in our heart. Since God is infinite wisdom and knowledge and we are limited, we know and prophesy in part. Nevertheless, we do know God in a manner sufficient for salvation and Christian living. When science points to technical accomplishment for persuasion, Christianity points to moral and spiritual accomplishment for persuasion. This provides the foundation for the right use of other knowledge.

Ours is also a hedonistic age that often lives by feeling while giving lip service to the publicly demonstrable truths of science. If it feels right and looks good to the individual, then it must be good. This often leads to moral anarchy in which each individual does what seems right in his own eyes. But feelings can change—and do regularly, as evidenced by the many broken marriages, friendships, and contracts in modern society.

Ours is also a violent age in which nations and factions seek to establish the truth of their political claims. The powerful suppress any evidence that conflicts with their position. The victors display the spoils with a vainglory meant to credit their position. Their attitude is that those who win the battle must be right. This has led to great social and global fragmentation.

Scientific theories disagree and often change. Feelings and personal preferences come and go. Those who are in power today are out of power tomorrow. This leads to doubt and despair in the hearts of millions of men and women who search for a firm basis on which to build their lives. In relation to the question before us, that of evidence for spiritual fullness, we must produce evidence that is publicly compelling (according to the Scriptures), privately fulfilling (addressing our doubts and satisfying the soul), and politically viable (able to overcome the tremendous spiritual opposition which comes on every hand to the cause of Christ).

Pentecostals assert that these are the last days, citing Acts 2 and Joel 2. They believe the great outpouring which initiated and carried forward the Pentecostal Movement of the 20th century is a sign of the soon coming of the Lord. The end is near, and this end is both a judgment of the present activity of the church and world and a goal that fills believers with hope and pulls them toward the Second Coming. Pentecostals live in a tension between what God has already done in Jesus Christ and what is not yet consummated. The kingdom of God—a kingdom of righteousness, joy, and peace in the Holy Spirit—is already at work among us. But it has not yet come in all its fullness. God reigns and rules in our hearts, but we long for the day when everything will be "holiness unto the Lord" and God will be all and in all.

If ours is a scientific, hedonistic, and violent age seen against the horizon of the soon coming of the Lord, what is the condition of the church? God calls forth and maintains the church, but it is also true that churches are broken, divided, and too often competitive. The church is being renewed in the Holy Spirit around the world, but it is also in danger of apostasy. Like the churches in the Book of Revelation, Jesus has commendations and warnings for today's church. The division and competitiveness of the church make it even more difficult for individuals to consider and weigh the evidence for being a Christian, especially a Spirit-filled Christian. Too often churches are not places where people can study the Word of God and test various doctrinal claims. Churches can appear to be like filling stations seeking only to pump blessings at a cheaper price than their competitors. Or they can be like circuses that bill acts and seek only to thrill crowds. Some churches are like nightclubs seeking to book headliners who will develop a loyal clientele of customers. Other churches seem to be reduced to mere schools for the development of the skills needed to cope with modern society but which provide no real community.

The church must be a place where everything is tested by the Scriptures and where people seek to be led by the Spirit and live from His fullness. If a church is not a missionary community actively engaged in evangelism and engaging the spiritual forces of darkness, the language of spiritual fullness will seem strange indeed. In other words, the context in which one searches can decisively shape the outcome of that search.

In North America, according to various formal and informal polls, the number of Spirit baptisms and those who claim to regularly speak in tongues or manifest spiritual gifts is going down. Perhaps boredom and cynicism are settling in. There are many reasons for this, but it must be remembered that the power of the Holy Spirit is given in order to be witnesses unto Christ. If the church that is claiming to be Spirit-filled is not a missionary community that is living with a sense of urgency, then its members will be caught up in the rush to respectability and social accommodation. People who continue to experience speaking in tongues in this context can actually be inoculated against it and other gifts because it seems so one-dimensional and self-serving.

Conflicting Evidence

The church exists in a world in which there are many spiritual counterfeits. Behavior similar to speaking in tongues is not limited to the Christian church. It never was. Other religions have prophetic claims and point to miraculous occurrences. If this isn't confusing enough, there is plenty of evidence of works of the flesh among those who claim to be filled with the Spirit. This conflicting evidence is confusing to the honest seeker and can be deadly to those who are wavering in their faith. Believers need to be reminded that it is not what they have but who has them that is important. It is not how much of the Spirit you have but how much of you the Spirit has. The point is to live from the fullness of God and not from the flesh, the world, or the devil's schemes.

But in addition to the carnality of Christians and the counterfeits of other religions and cults, Christians disagree among themselves as to the significance of Spirit baptism. Most non-Pentecostal Evangelicals say baptism in the Holy Spirit occurs at conversion, when the believer is baptized into Christ. Many maintain that the sign gifts of the apostolic age ceased at that time. Writers such as John F. MacArthur, Jr., continue to write books promoting this position. What is disconcerting is not that they state these contrary positions but that their books seem to evidence no engagement with Pentecostal scholarship. Roman Catholics have a significant number of members who are involved in the Charismatic renewal. For Catholics, the baptism in the Holy Spirit is a release of the sacramental grace given in baptism. As such it is a realization of their Christian initiation. But the baptism in the Holy Spirit is not the normal expectation prescribed by the church for every believer. Lutherans like Larry Christenson are influential Charismatic teachers. But most Lutherans are very suspicious of Pentecostal spirituality and largely regard it as a kind of enthusiasm, if not a legalistic religion, that requires certain conditions for receiving the filling of the Spirit. So-called Third Wave Charismatics (John Wimber, Peter Wagner, et. al.) emphasize power encounters in which persons are healed and demons are expelled. They reject the teaching that speaking in tongues is the initial evidence of Holy Spirit baptism. They regard tongues as one gift among many, but not having the significance ascribed to it by Pentecostals.

If the foregoing represent conflicting claims, there are also gross contradictions of spiritual fullness. These contradictions are the sins against the Holy Spirit which deserve serious consideration by anyone who is seeking to weigh the evidence and to hold fast to what is true. These sins include grieving the Spirit (Ephesians 4:30), quenching the Spirit (1 Thessalonians 5:19), insulting the Spirit (Hebrews 10:26-29), resisting the Spirit (Acts 7:51), lying to the Spirit (Acts 5:1-11), and blasphemy against the Holy Spirit (Matthew 12:31, 32). Any claims to spiritual fullness are contradicted by the manifestation of any of these sins against the Spirit, whereas the opposite of these sins is consistent with the spiritual life.

The context of Ephesians 4:30 (vv. 25-32) indicates that believers may grieve the Holy Spirit by their dispositions, deeds, and discourse. Lying, anger, and grudges give opportunity to the devil. Members must quit their former sins, stealing for example. No evil talk is to come out of the believer's mouth, but only what is useful for edification so that words may minister grace to those who hear. Bitterness, wrath, anger, arguing, and slander, along with all malice, grudges, and evil intent, must be put away, and believers must forgive with a tender heart and kindness. Tearing down the body of Christ with our disposition, deeds, and discourse grieves the Spirit; building up the body of Christ pleases God the Holy Spirit.

The context of 1 Thessalonians 5:19 (vv. 16-22) indicates that the opposite of quenching the Spirit is to rejoice always, pray without ceasing, and to give thanks in all things. Those who are thus disposed toward God will not despise prophetic utterances, thus the complacency, indifference, and apathy of the world will be overcome in one who is aflame with the Spirit and burns brightly and clearly as a witness for Christ.

According to Hebrews 10:26-29, the Spirit of God is insulted or outraged when a believer willfully persists in sin after having received the knowledge of the truth. One who violated the law of Moses died without mercy on the testimony of two or three witnesses. The writer of Hebrews was asking, "What will be the end of those who have spurned the Son of God and profaned the blood of the covenant, which is the basis of their sanctification?" Those who claim to be Spirit-filled while willfully persisting in known sin contradict their claim, and whatever evidence they have otherwise is undermined. The Spirit is honored when the believer follows His leading into all truth and manifests the character of Christ, who came to do the will of the Father.

In Acts 7:51, Stephen accused his fellow Jewish hearers of resisting the Holy Spirit as their fathers had done when they had rejected the warnings of the prophets. By rejecting Jesus Christ they were resisting the witness and the leading of the Holy Spirit. Those who refuse to acknowledge and yield to the Holy Spirit resist His work and cannot know and live from His fullness. The Holy Spirit does not possess a person as demons do. He enables, leads, and convinces. The Christian life is not an inevitability. It is a yielding and a seeking after God and His will for our life. All we need is found in Christ by the Spirit, and God is working in us "both to will and to do of his good pleasure." But we must "work out [our] salvation with fear and trembling" (Philippians 2:12, 13).

In Acts 5:1-11, Ananias and Sapphira lied to the Holy Spirit by pretending to give all while holding back a portion of their property. They sinned against the Holy Spirit, who is the source of unity in Christian community. The Spirit of life struck them dead. The Holy Spirit is serious about Christian fellowship, and those who do not discern the body of Christ are subject to spiritual sickness and death (1 Corinthians 10; 11:30).

Finally, in Matthew 12:31, 32, Jesus said that speaking against the Son is forgivable while blasphemy against the Holy Spirit is not. This is not because the Holy Spirit is more divine than Jesus Christ. It is because no one may know the true identity of Jesus and be conformed to Him apart from the work of the Holy Spirit. When someone rejects His witness, they have rejected the only means whereby one may know and follow Jesus Christ. They have attributed evil to the One who is good and the source of goodness. The Holy Spirit is to be blessed and honored, and His witness is to be accredited before the watching world. When believers fail to honor the Holy

Spirit or by their words and actions trivialize His work among them, they take steps toward denying His witness. Blasphemy against the Spirit is not something that someone does spontaneously. Usually a process involving the previously discussed sins against the Spirit culminates in the ultimate sin against the Holy Spirit—blasphemy. If a person persists in this sin, he cannot be forgiven, because he rejects the Spirit who brings conviction. The Holy Spirit strives to embody in the church and each believer the witness to Jesus Christ. Jesus, who overcame sin in the flesh, desires that we should glorify God in our flesh. Every spirit that denies that Jesus is come in the flesh, that denies the Incarnation, that denies the person and character and work of Jesus is not of God. The point of the admonition in 1 John 4:1-3, 15 is that we should test the spirits to see whether they are of God. When we love and obey Jesus Christ from the heart, we are living proof, an evidence, a witness, that is consistent with the witness of the Holy Spirit. Those who are filled with the Spirit seek to fill the world around them with this witness.

Spiritual Evidence

In speaking of evidence of spiritual baptism, it is important to discuss the fullness of "whom." Many discussions about evidence start with the "what" or the effects rather than the person, character, and work of the Holy Spirit. Evidence of spiritual fullness must be spiritual evidence; that is, it must be evidence that is a fruit and manifestation of the Holy Spirit. The Holy Spirit is a person who never possesses or dominates as an evil spirit does. The Holy

Spirit is not an inner aspect of the person. The spirit of the prophet is subject to the prophet (see 1 Corinthians 14:32), but the Holy Spirit is subject to no one. The Holy Spirit is a person and therefore His work is personal and produces persons who act in loving freedom to accomplish God's will.

The Holy Spirit is pure and will not dwell in an unclean temple. Those who claim to be filled with the Spirit while living defiled lives and defiling others contradict their claim. This is why early Pentecostals wanted to keep the association of sanctification and Spirit baptism. Indeed the Holiness Movement of the 19th century came to equate entire sanctification and baptism in the Holy Spirit. Purity and power were two sides of the same coin for them. Early Pentecostals maintained that the Holy Spirit would be poured out upon a consecrated vessel *emptied* of carnal desires and resistances to God so that it might be *filled* with the Holy Spirit. The power of the Holy Spirit will not move one to act in ways which contradict Scripture. The Holy Spirit inspired the Bible. Therefore, if He led someone to contradict Scripture, He would be contradicting Himself. The Holy Spirit has real power—power to accomplish God's purposes in the world. The Holy Spirit is God. Therefore the Spirit will never glorify an individual or a church; rather, the individual or church that is filled with the Spirit will glorify God in character and deeds.

The Holy Spirit moved on holy men of God who wrote the Holy Scriptures and were a part of the community of saints—the holy ones! (2 Peter 1:21). The writers of Holy Scripture knew the truth and therefore were free to walk in the light. They spoke the truth in love and thus built up the church and helped to equip the believers for every good and perfect work in the ministry of the whole people of God. It is possible to make claims to spiritual fullness and lie with one's deeds. If a person's deeds are not scriptural and his motive is something other than love, then he is not acting in the truth. Truth was related to the faithfulness and dependability of God in the Old Testament and to the freedom which God would give through the gospel of Jesus Christ in the New Testament era (John 8:32). Those who are filled with the Spirit will love the truth and search the Scriptures in order to walk in all the light the Spirit shines on their path (1 John 1:7).

The early Pentecostals did not condemn other believers for not seeking to be filled with the Spirit in the way they were, or for failing to speak in tongues and manifest spiritual gifts. Rather, they testified that they must walk in all the light God had revealed to them. And they made the claim that this was indeed scriptural. Those who are filled with the Spirit will walk according to the Scriptures and will love every other believer in Christ. They will embrace the fullness of fruit and gifts as the way of faithful witness in the world, the way in which truth is made known in word and power and demonstration of the Holy Spirit.

Pentecostals believe that apostolic succession is evidenced by those who live from and demonstrate the same power and Spirit that Jesus' apostles manifested in their witness. God the Father, who sent the Son and poured out the Holy Spirit, inspired the Scriptures and called forth a people who would live from God's fullness and manifest His character and deeds to a watching world.

Being filled with the Spirit and speaking in tongues is not supposed to be a terminal experience! The testimony of early Pentecostals indicates they were on a holy journey. They were walking in the light and following Jesus in obedience, sanctification, and Spirit-filled witness. They were sent into the world as He was sent. One needs only to listen to the early Pentecostal songs to get a sense of this movement of the Spirit in the lives of those who were living from the fullness. This is illustrated in songs like "I Feel Like Traveling On" or "Marching to Zion." The filling with the Holy Spirit constitutes the church as a missionary movement that powerfully engages movements animated by other spirits and based on doctrines of demons. Anything good or beautiful or true that may be observed anywhere in the world is the result of the activity of the Spirit of God. Wherever men and women receive the witness of the Spirit to goodness, truth, and beauty, they will, upon hearing the gospel, recognize the true Lord and Savior of the world—Jesus Christ.

All that has been said up to this point is meant to teach that there is a lot more to Pentecostals than speaking in tongues. There is a lot more, but no less!

Initial Evidence

Outsiders quickly labeled modern-day Pentecostalism "the tongues movement." Some Pentecostals seeking to move away from what seemed to them a narrow focus on tongues have downplayed the initial evidence and speaking of tongues as *an* evidence, or *one among many* evidences. While it is true that speaking in tongues must be seen within the whole picture (the gestalt) of the Christian life lived in the last days, it is important not to lose sight of the significance of speaking in tongues for Spirit baptism.

In Acts 2, the cloven tongues were distributed to every believer in the Upper Room, and they all spoke in tongues. In Acts 9 Paul was filled with the Spirit and later told the Corinthian church that he thanked God he spoke in tongues more than all of them (1 Corinthians 14:18). It was Paul's desire that they all speak in tongues (v. 5). While noting abuses in the Corinthian church, Paul nevertheless commanded them, "Forbid not to speak with tongues" (v. 39). In Acts 10 and 11 is the account and explanation of the outpouring of the Spirit on the household of Cornelius. Peter said they received the Spirit just as the apostles had on the Day of Pentecost, "for they heard them speak with tongues" (Acts 10:46, 47). This is what Pentecostals maintain today. As believers in the gospel, their hearts have been purified by faith, they have been filled with the Holy Spirit, and they "speak with new tongues" (Mark 16:17). In Acts 19:1-7, the Ephesian believers were filled with the Holy Spirit and spoke in tongues and prophesied. Pentecostals do not maintain that those who are filled with the Spirit will only speak in tongues; they simply maintain that this is the initial evidence.

Speaking in tongues should not be divorced from other forms of prayer. Christians pray with words understood, without words (sighs and groans), and with words not understood but nevertheless meaningful (speaking in tongues). These three modes of prayer are mutually conditioning. As one hears the gospel and is taught in the Scriptures, he comes to understand his life in terms of the scriptural story. The believer's prayers are to be structured by the Word of God. All prayer is to be in the Spirit who inspired the Scriptures and helps each believer to pray. As the believer's understanding is shaped and directed by the Word of God, he or she prays prayers of thanksgiving, praise, and intercession. Sometimes the burden for lost and hurting people becomes so great that the Spirit of God will sigh within the believer, who also groans and longs for the salvation and healing of all those in the world. The fullness of the Holy Spirit does not always issue in laughter. Tears may also be evidence of the filling with the Holy Spirit. The body is built up through both tears and joy. Spirit-filled worship will have a place for weeping as well as rejoicing. When the Spirit sheds the love of God abroad in the heart of the believer, that love turns to compassion in the context of the many sheep who are scattered without a shepherd and of those whom Satan is seeking to devour as a ravenous wolf or a roaring lion.

A mind shaped by the Word of God and a heart affected by the love of God will seek to express in prayer, praise, and proclamation the mighty acts of God. Believers who meditate upon the Word, long for the coming of the Lord, and yield to the probing of the Holy Spirit become vessels of service in the Lord's kingdom.

Every community in the world is characterized by a certain language. On the Day of Pentecost, those gathered in Jerusalem heard the disciples telling the mighty acts of God in their own languages. Speaking in tongues, whether in known or unknown languages (Acts 2; 1 Corinthians 14), is speech that is enabled by the Holy Spirit. It is eschatological speech, words which indicate the last days are upon us. The power of the world to come is manifested in this world by such speech. Regular human speech is transcended, for when we speak in tongues our spirit prays as the Spirit initiates speech. Speaking in tongues becomes a paradigm or a model of Christian witness in word and power and demonstration of the Spirit. Believers speak as they yield to and are enabled by the Holy Spirit.

The indwelling Spirit leads all Christians into the truth and teaches them what they need to know of Jesus Christ. The filling with the Spirit will simply realize the intended purpose of the indwelling—that every believer should be a Christlike witness in the power of the Holy Spirit.

John the Baptist was filled with the Spirit and leapt in his mother's womb; Zacharias was filled with the Spirit and prophesied. It is the privilege of believers from Pentecost forward to speak with other tongues as the Spirit gives utterance. In this way, believers give expression to the inexpressible.

People who are filled with the Spirit do not claim they are more mature or more knowledgeable in the Scriptures than other Christians. Those who are filled with the Spirit have no inherent claim to superiority that can be sustained by the Scriptures. However, they all testify to walking in the light that God has shined on their paths. They all testify to the fact that their Christian lives are better and stronger and that they are more effective in their witness than they were before. If a believer did not think that being filled with the Holy Spirit was better than not being filled, why would he or she seek it?

Being filled with the Spirit should never be a source of division in the church. It will only become so if those who are filled with the Spirit and speak in other tongues are forced out of a church, or if they make erroneous claims and become puffed up in pride.

Pentecostals are often asked, "But do I have to speak in tongues to be filled with the Spirit?" When I was asked this question in the early 1970s as an urban missionary in Atlanta, Georgia, my response was that you did not have to kiss the bride or the groom in order to be married. But if one understands what a kiss is and what marriage is, one does not ask, "Do I have to?" Kissing has significance only within the covenant of marriage and the larger meaning of life. Marriage is a holy covenant that testifies to the relationship between Christ and the church. As such, kissing is a symbol of the affection between a husband and wife. Lips touch lips, and love is not simply symbolized but mediated, expressed, enhanced. Speaking in tongues is a privilege of every Spirit-filled believer. Like a kiss it can be faked or, as in the case of Judas, signify betrayal instead of affection. But the counterfeit does not disprove the real. On the contrary, it proves that there is a genuine article.

Speaking in tongues is not the power, it is evidence of the Spirit's filling. But it is also empowering since believers joyously participate in Holy Spirit-enabled speech that is deeply meaningful though not understood in the usual sense. The believer's spirit prays.

This personal edification is important in a day of spiritual weakness and oppression. Here is a language no person or demon can decipher or deflect. It is the language of the kingdom of God. In this way, members of God's good creation, restored through Jesus Christ, already participate in the age to come and pray down the power of the future Kingdom into the present.

But some Pentecostals and Charismatics have been so zealous for tongues as to make the same mistake as their detractors. They in effect have reduced the filling of the Spirit to speaking in tongues. Thus, in some quarters, people are taught to speak in tongues! That is illegitimate and self-defeating. Even worse, when a person who has been taught to speak in tongues encounters real demons and opposition to the gospel, he will not have the power which the Spirit alone can provide to overcome and be a faithful witness. Some misguided and unscrupulous individuals may teach people to speak in tongues in order to count them in a perverted competition to see how many spiritual experiences can be induced. Such tongues are not enabled by the Holy Spirit; and even if they are meant to help the chronic seeker overcome his or her reluctance to speak, the end result will be a discouraged, disappointed, and even embittered person.

People can be taught to speak in tongues as a natural phenomenon. They can speak in tongues as a result of the influence of evil spirits, or they can speak in tongues as they are enabled by the Holy Spirit. The true filling with the Holy Spirit will produce a witness to Jesus Christ in word, power, and demonstration of the Spirit. In a context of loving consecration, joyous praise, and missionary faithfulness, a Spirit-filled believer is produced and maintained.

I shall never forget, as a little boy, hearing my mother intercede in tongues, groan in the Spirit, and sing as the Spirit filled her heart and mind. She knew much sorrow and came through many difficulties in her life, but as she would "pray through" and the Spirit would come upon her, her countenance and her voice would take on a beauty and strength not of this world. Millions of poor, disenfranchised people throughout the world, who have been told that their voice does not count and that they have nothing to contribute, by the power of the Holy Spirit are given a voice and become victors instead of victims. They become witnesses to Jesus Christ in a divine drama in which they are now key players. These individuals, like my mother and father, find comfort and strength in the Holy Spirit for a vocation of witness to Jesus Christ. They are actors in the drama of redemption, and their lives are thus given new significance and meaning.

Speaking in tongues is the evidence of the filling with the Spirit, an eschatological sign of the last days, a source of personal edification to the believer, a gift to be interpreted for the edification of the body of Christ, and a means of underscoring the difference between the church and the world. Speaking in tongues is not law but gospel. It is not the cause of the baptism in the Holy Spirit; it is the evidence. But it is not the only evidence; and when it is the only evidence, it is not evidence of the filling with the Spirit.

Essential Evidence

As speaking in tongues is an effect of Spirit filling, love is a manifestation of the character of God. Love is the source or fountain of all the other fruit of the Spirit. Paul told the church at Corinth (1 Corinthians 13) that one may speak in tongues, have mountain-moving faith, understand all mysteries, have all knowledge, give one's goods for relief of the poor, and give one's body in sacrificial service—but without love it profits nothing!

Love is the word we use to symbolize the mutual self-giving which we see in the divine Trinity. Into this life of self-giving the believer is taken by the Holy Spirit through Jesus Christ in the love of the Father. God so loved the world that He gave His Son. The Son gave up His life as a ransom for many. The Holy Spirit gives His life to bear witness to Jesus Christ and to comfort all believers.

Without love we may try to develop the inner and outer characteristics of the other *fruits* of the Spirit, but it is love which makes these characteristics into *fruit* of the Spirit. Love is the inner content of our union with God in Christ by the Holy Spirit. Love fulfills the law of God and is the motive for all obedience. Believers walk in all the light God sheds on their path because they love God. Love keeps believers from competing with each other in the church and assures that believers will not grade the gifts and those who manifest the gifts according to some carnal scale of self-glorification. Fruit and gifts belong together as do character and personality in an individual's life.

To know God is to love God, and to love God is to

love others. Love is the inner meaning of sanctification and Christian perfection. Those who love God with all their being will love their neighbor and will reach out to the lost and hurting. Love becomes the motive for seeking the baptism in the Holy Spirit. Love is not power, but it is the motive for seeking God for the strength to give an effectual witness in the face of the demonic forces opposing the gospel of Jesus Christ in today's world. Love is the motive for the ultimate evidence of the baptism in the Holy Spirit.

Ultimate Evidence

The writer of Hebrews said that Jesus by the eternal Spirit made an offering of Himself (9:14). John said the meaning of love is found not in the fact that we have loved God but that God first loved us and gave Himself for us (1 John 4:10). It is this sacrificial love that is the motive and heart of true witness. The baptism in the Holy Spirit is not meant to issue in words alone, however forcefully delivered. In fact, volume and force have nothing to do with it. The word for *witness* in the New Testament (*marturia*) is the one from which we derive the word *martyr*. Christian witness is a life-and-death matter. More men and women have given their lives in the service of the gospel in this century than in any previous century of recorded history.

Speaking in tongues is communication with the Commander in Chief, the Lord of Hosts, who leads His church as an army into battle and calls upon soldiers of the Cross to give themselves daily as lambs among wolves. This is not something a parent would lightly desire for his or her children. Indeed, consecration and filling with the Holy Spirit will mean that our children will be involved in suffering and conflict with the world and the devil until Jesus comes again. But it is far better to suffer for righteousness' sake, for love's sake, or for Christ's sake than to suffer as an evildoer or a carnal Christian who avoids the way of the Cross.

In Matthew 16:24 Jesus said, "If any man will come after me, let him deny himself, and take up his cross, and follow me." The way of discipleship is the way of self-sacrificing witness. This is not something that any one of us does naturally. It can only be the fruit of the power of the Holy Spirit who enabled Jesus to offer Himself on Calvary.

The ultimate goal of Pentecostal believers is not to make an apology for speaking in tongues; it is to give their life in service for the Master. All prayer—whether with words, sighs, or tongues—is to be in the Spirit. And all prayer is vital for Christian witnesses who must maintain communication with the Lord of Hosts, who alone can give direction, comfort, and strength in the spiritual battles to which the church is called today. When the Spirit speaks with such immediacy in the speech of the believer, there is a sacramental mediation, a making visible of the power of the age to come and the grace of the Lord Jesus. The humblest believer is therefore enabled to pray with sighs too deep for words and with longing and joy to press forward to the prize of the high calling in Christ Jesus.

Conclusion

In a scientific, hedonistic, and violent age, Spirit-filled believers will seek to give evidence of the full-ness and provision of God through walking in the light, walking in love, and walking in the power of the Holy Spirit. They will test all things by the Scriptures and hold fast to what is good. Discernment of spirits, which is a gift of the Holy Spirit, will oper-ate in any church that will search the Scriptures and seek to live in missionary faithfulness in the last days. Such a church will test spiritual manifestations by ask-ing the following questions: Is this consistent with the fruit of the Spirit? Does this honor Jesus Christ? Is this scriptural? Does this build up the body of Christ? Does this provoke the body of Christ to right-eousness? Does this further the church's mission?

Since we prophesy and know in part, there will be occasions when our fallible, weak humanity—and, yes, even our carnality—will distort or garble the message God is trying to speak to us. But the same God who graciously bestows His gifts will also gra-ciously judge, chastise, and discipline us so that we may be clearer witnesses of Jesus Christ.

The baptism in the Holy Spirit with the initial evi-dence of speaking in other tongues is by grace through faith. Like everything good, it is the gift of God. This power is God's gift to the whole church. It is poured out upon the sanctified life for last-days missionary service. This sanctification is not merely positional, imputed righteousness. Nor is it gradual growth, though that is a part of the sanctified life. Sanctification begins with a real change in the heart at regeneration when the believer is set apart from the world and joined to Christ. The sanctification which should be associated with the baptism in the Holy

Spirit is a result of cleansing and mortification of the deeds of the flesh until the heart is perfect in love. This purity of heart is the center of Christian spirituality and the motive for the believer's walk in righteousness and his or her seeking continually to be filled with the Holy Spirit in order to witness to a lost and hurting world. This wholehearted love is a daily gift of the Savior to all those for whom He prayed in John 17, and it is their greatest gift to Him.

Pentecostals do not believe they have all the truth or that they are the only ones going to heaven. We struggle to share with our brothers and sisters throughout the body of Christ the wonderful, glorious, inexpressible blessings, comfort, and power of the Holy Spirit which He has made known to us through Christ. In the face of the counterfeits surrounding the body of Christ and the apostasy and false doctrine from within, Pentecostals seek to be faithful to the purpose for which God has raised them up. They seek to be a blessing to the church and a witness to the world in word and power and in demonstration of the Holy Spirit.

The church, as it is meant to be, is the body of Christ, "the fullness of Him who fills all in all" (Ephesians 1:23, *NKJV*). Those who are filled with the Holy Spirit live from this fullness of God, made known and given in and through Jesus Christ. One day God will be all and in all. Until that day, let us keep on being filled with the Holy Spirit!

Bibliography

Arrington, French L. *Christian Doctrine: A Pentecostal Perspective*, Vol. 3. Cleveland, Tenn.: Pathway Press, 1994.

Ervin, Howard M. *Spirit Baptism: A Biblical Investigation*. Peabody, Mass.: Hendrickson Publishers, Inc., 1987.

___. *Conversion-Initiation in the Baptism in the Holy Spirit: An Engaging Critique of James D.G. Dunn's Baptism in the Holy Spirit*. Peabody, Mass.: Hendrickson Publishers, nc., 1984.

___. *These Are Not Drunken As Ye Suppose*. Plainfield, N.J.: Logos, 1968.

Gause, R. Hollis. *Living in the Spirit: The Way of Salvation*. Cleveland, Tenn.: Pathway Press, 1980.

Higgins, John R., Michael L. Dusing and Frank D. Tollman. *Introduction to Theology: A Classical Pentecostal Perspective*. Dubuque, Iowa; Kendall/Hunt Publishing Co., 1993.

Horton, Wade H., gen. ed. *The Glossolalia Phenomenon*. Cleveland, Tenn.: Pathway Press, 1966.

Hughes, Ray H., ed. *Who Is the Holy Ghost?* Cleveland, Tenn.: Pathway Press, 1992.

Land, Steven J. *Pentecostal Spirituality: A Passion for the Kingdom*. Sheffield, England: Sheffield Academic Press, 1993.

Macchia, Frank. "Sighs Too Deep for Words." *Journal of Pentecostal Theology, Issue* 1 (October 1992), pp. 47-73.

Synan, Vinson, ed. *Aspects of Pentecostal-Charismatic Origins.* Plainfield, N.J.: Logos International, 1975.

Underwood, B.E. *The Gifts of the Spirit: Supernatural Equipment for Christian Service.* Franklin Springs, Ga.: Advocate Press, 1967.

The Holy Spirit's Work in the Church

4

Dr. Oliver L. McMahan is assistant professor of pastoral care and counseling at the Church of God School of Theology in Cleveland, Tennessee.

Dr. McMahan is the assistant director of the Western School of Christian Ministry. He was associate professor of Bible, dean of students, and pastor of the Total Life Center at Northwest Bible College in Minot, North Dakota. He is a member of the Executive Council of the Church of God.

Oliver McMahan

Understanding the Holy Spirit's work in the church is vital for Pentecostals because Pentecost is wedded to the Holy Spirit. The very term *Pentecostal* comes from biblical accounts of the Old Testament Feast of Pentecost and of the work of the Holy Spirit on the Day of Pentecost. Blindly calling yourself a Pentecostal without seeking to understand scriptural insights about the Spirit is to invite heresy and spiritual disaster. God's work through the Holy Spirit in the church is His primary means for revealing who He is in the world.

The meaning of the church, especially the Spirit-filled church, is found in the work of the Holy Spirit. Without the Spirit operating in the church, churches are religious clubs meeting on Sundays, not biblical congregations. Remove the Spirit and all that remains is a shell of words and teachings, barren of God-breathed life. Neglect the power of the Spirit and the church is left to be overrun by the pressures of society and the warfare in the spirit world.

The Holy Spirit may be understood as the chief executive officer of the church, manifesting Himself in many operational modes. The Holy Spirit is at the center of all that the church is and does—rather than just something that happens occasionally. The operation of the Spirit is not a tradition seeking to recapture a reality that passed with another church era. The gifts of the Spirit move like a mighty, overwhelming wind to this very day, anticipating the very coming of the Lord.

The Holy Spirit as Source and Center of God's Action in the Church
1 Corinthians 12:1-6

Avoiding Idolatrous Worship

"Now concerning spiritual gifts, brethren, I would not have you ignorant. Ye know that ye were Gentiles, carried away unto these dumb idols, even as ye were led" (1 Corinthians 12:1, 2).

Understanding the Holy Spirit and His work is the plea of Paul in 1 Corinthians 12. The core of that understanding deals with idolatry. Without a clear focus on the God of the gifts, worship either shifts to the gifts themselves or the gifts are used in the service of some demigod or superficial personality.

Learning about the Spirit means being profoundly aware of the leading of the Spirit. The leading of the Spirit of God is the key to worship, not what we attempt to generate in a worship service. The focus of the operation of the Spirit is Christ. Though His work within us is powerful, we are led not by our experiences—even experiences of the Spirit—but by the Spirit himself.

The Word of God is important for combating ignorance about the operation of the Holy Spirit, since both the Word and we are illuminated by the Holy Spirit. The standard for interpreting and understanding the work of the Spirit must be the Word. This chapter will look at important Scripture texts in 1 Corinthians 12—14, Acts 2, and Ephesians 5 to understand how the Spirit moves within the church.

By the Spirit

"Wherefore I give you to understand, that no man speaking by the Spirit of God calleth Jesus accursed: and that no man can say that Jesus is the Lord, but by the Holy Ghost. Now there are diversities of gifts, but the same Spirit. And there are differences of administrations, but the same Lord. And there are diversities of operations, but it is the same God which worketh all in all" (1 Corinthians 12:3-6).

"By the Spirit" rings as a phrase of correction. Lest there should be any doubt about the source of the operations of the Spirit, Paul steered his readers to see that the manifestations occurring in their churches were from God—"by the Spirit." The Holy Spirit is the divine personal agent by whom Christ as the head of the church communicates and activates the authentic work of the church.

Modern-version Pentecostalism readily follows "gifted" individuals, trendy forms of worship, or provocative teachings. The Holy Spirit is crowded to the sidelines as the church pursues an experience rather than

God. In verses 3-11, Paul stressed 11 times that the operation of the Spirit is from the Spirit. We are to follow the Spirit; the Spirit does not follow us.

"By the Spirit," "same Spirit," "same Lord," and "same God" are all used to convey that God is the originating source and directing center of the church's action. Becoming a Christian and confessing Christ as Lord begins and is guided by the Spirit. "Gifts"—divine empowerments for discipleship and service—may differ but are all guided by the Spirit. "Administrations"—the application and supervision of God's work—are diverse but all come under the guid0ations"—the actual functions of the work of God—are different, but all occur only because of the initiative of God.

The Goal of the Spirit: Edifying the Body
1 Corinthians 12:7-13; Ephesians 5:18-21;
Acts 2:1-13

Edifying the Body

"But the manifestation of the Spirit is given to every man to profit withal" (1 Corinthians 12:7).

Gifts are not isolated entitlements to do whatever the gifted person wants to do with them. Fellow believers in the body of Christ are as much a part of the gift as the person exercising it. A person receives a gift not for himself only, but for the body as well. "To profit withal"—meaning "for the profit of all"—leaves little room for elitist, specialized, closed-group applications, much less self-centered benefits. "Manifestation" refers to a perceptible work of the Spirit. With the *giving*, the Spirit chooses the *profit*.

Various Gifts From the Spirit

"For to one is given by the Spirit the word of wisdom; to another the word of knowledge by the same Spirit; to another faith by the same Spirit; to another the gifts of healing by the same Spirit; to another the working of miracles; to another prophecy; to another discerning of spirits; to another divers kinds of tongues; to another the interpretation of tongues" (1 Corinthians 12:8-10).

Given is the most important word in this passage for learning the operation of the Spirit. The source of the gift is more important than the substance of the gift. The content of the gift is important, but it is secondary to the creator of the gift. A gift is identified as a gift of the Spirit because of the Spirit, not because of the substance of the gift.

The Giver, more than the gift, should attract the adoration of the church. We gravitate to the gift, seeking to use it rather than to be used. Stewardship of the gifts God has given was the intention of Paul as he instructed the church about the operation of the gifts.

By contrast, the church, teachers, preachers, seminar speakers, and a plethora of advocates—composing something akin to a movement—bear a conviction that knowing your gift and becoming empowered for service is the goal of the Spirit-filled life. With so much emphasis upon "my gift" and possession of a gift, the emphasis can easily shift from God to us, and priority can move from knowing the gift giver to using the gift.

"By the Spirit" was Paul's message. The existence

of gifts was assumed. That every Spirit-filled believer
is used was vital. But the church needed to hear
what made the gift possible. The phrase "by the
Spirit," or its equivalent, was used by Paul six times in
verses 3-11. In verse 8, the first usage of "by" is the
Greek term *dia*. The emphasis is that the originating
cause, that which brought the gift into existence, is
the Spirit. In the second usage in verse 8, "by" is
from the Greek word *kata*. The emphasis is that the
Spirit is the guiding or dominating Person, assuring
that the operation is genuine.

The most extensive and direct list of spiritual gifts
is found in these verses. The content of the gifts can
be studied by looking at the terms used to list the
gifts of the Spirit. The terms bear an indication of
what God is doing when He gives a spiritual gift to a
Spirit-filled believer. Since Paul did not actually give
full definitions, modern-day definitions must measure
their speculations by the names and terms Paul actually used in listing the gifts.

The spiritual gifts Paul listed in 1 Corinthians 12:8-
10 are word of wisdom, word of knowledge, faith,
gifts of healing, working of miracles, prophecy, discerning of spirits, divers (different) kinds of tongues,
and the interpretation of tongues. Later in the chapter (vv. 28-30), he mentioned gifts of healings, workers of miracles, interpretation, and diversities (vari-
eties) of tongues. He also listed what have tradition-
ally been called offices—apostles, prophets, and
teachers. Further, he named helps and governments
(administrations). All of these gifts have been given
by God, as opposed to something earned or self-
developed.

Word of wisdom. Word indicates the formation and articulation of spoken communication. Not only the content but also the intent is implied. Wisdom came from the Greek term *sophia,* which emphasizes ability, skill, and insight. A word of wisdom is a word from God that gives insight and direction.

Word of knowledge. Knowledge comes from a Greek term that emphasizes information and relationship. The information is important, and the context from which it comes is also important. Word of knowledge indicates information that reflects relationship with God. The information enhances one's relationship with God.

The gift of *faith. Faith* as a gift of the Spirit is to be distinguished from the faith (believing) required to be a Christian. The emphasis as a gift is upon divine origin and enablement that transcends creedal content. It is a special enablement to believe "faith claims" of the Bible on the basis of divine promise. Extra faith is not necessarily given. Rather, the divine origin of one's faith for something or someone is especially real and present.

Gifts of healing. Healing indicates supernatural intervention to bring a change in the circumstance of a person, especially as it relates to physical health, so that illness is removed, sickness is remedied, broken limbs are repaired, and diseased organs are restored.

Working of miracles does not imply that the person being used by the Spirit produces the manifestation. The emphasis is upon an actual change, a work that is done. Rather than a change of mind or an abstraction, a change in natural, normal processes takes place. "Working" in this text comes from a Greek term with roots similar to the term *energy* (*energe-ma*). The word translated "miracle" has similarities with the term *power* (*dunamis*).

Prophecy refers to the speaking forth of a message from God. The content of the message is powerful, and the substance may refer to either present or future information; however, the important thing to remember is that the message comes from God.

Discerning of spirits. *Discerning* comes from a compound Greek term that literally indicates distinguishing "through discretionary judgment." The word emphasizes the ability to determine the circumstance standing between different parts of a decision and then being able to make the decision. Ability to tell the truth regarding a spirit, person, or circumstance is also indicated. The emphasis is especially upon the unseen spirit realm.

Divers kinds of tongues. *Divers* means different; *kinds* indicates categories; *tongues* refers to languages. This gift is the ability from God to speak in different kinds of speech. The purpose of this gift is to focus attention upon communicating with God; that is, an individual or a body of believers becomes aware of a need to commune with God.

Interpretation of tongues. *Interpretation* (Greek, *hermeneia*, from which we get the English word *hermeneutics*) includes not just the meaning but also the intent of a communication. The full message of an interpretation is deeper than just a translation. The intended message comes across in the interpretation, while a translation may be devoid of the intent of the one originating the message.

Apostles, prophets, teachers, and workers of miracles are individuals through whom the gifts of the Spirit operate, though the operation of the Spirit is not limited to them. These are offices, functions, and roles that result from the working of the Spirit, all of which are manifested through individuals. They may or may not hold an official position. For example, someone through whom the Spirit operates to perform mighty miracles may not hold a specific office in the church in the same sense that a teacher holds a teaching office. Nevertheless, both the gift and the position originate from God.

An *apostle* (Greek, *apostolos*) is someone sent by God to accomplish a specific mission. He is one who has received a special commission for a precedent-setting task. Examples are establishing the apostles' doctrine as the original apostles did, being with the Lord physically as the original Twelve had been, or someone today reaching a country or people group that has never been reached before.

The word *prophet* (Greek, *prophetes*) is from a combination of two Greek terms *pro* and *phemi*, meaning "before, in front of" and "speaking." Thus, a prophet is someone who places in front of others a message from the Lord, which may refer to events in the future or divine insight about current events. The emphasis is upon the fact that the word spoken is from God. Whatever the message of the prophet by the manifestation of the Spirit, it always agrees with the Scripture.

A *teacher* is someone who by life and example instructs others. The reference is not merely to the abilitiy to communicate information but to bring to the hearers the life-changing message of Christ. The Spirit uses a person and the gifts He gives the individual, enabling him to teach with God-given profundity to affect the lives of others.

Workers of miracles refers to individuals gifted by God so that miracles are manifest in their ministries. The work accomplished is clearly supernatural in origin and effect. This may involve the alteration of the regular course of nature, the changing of a person's life circumstance, or some other event that supersedes the natural order of occurrence. The gift of working of miracles (1 Corinthians 12:10) was defined earlier in this chapter.

Helps (Greek, *antilempsis*) means to bring something to another. The Spirit uses a person to bring whatever is needed to supply the needs of others.

Governments emphasizes guidance and steering. The term is used to refer to administration and organizing. A person used of the Spirit in this capacity equips others and helps to implement their gifts for greater effectiveness.

In moving our attention to Paul's teaching on the operation of the Spirit and spiritual gifts, three points are important to keep in mind. First, though the greater amount of teaching is given to the Spirit's operation, Paul's foundational and central point is that the gift giver is the key to spiritual gifts. Second, the content of gifts is secondary in importance to the One who gives the gift—God. Finally, though Paul's teaching on the operation of the Spirit is extensive, his message is clear and straightforward: The Spirit gives gifts to individuals in the context of the church. If a person leaves the body of believers, he leaves the active flow of the manifestation of the Spirit. Also, a church that does not affirm the activity of the Spirit within individuals in gifts and manifestations grieves the Spirit.

The attention of Paul shifts after verse 10 from God as the giver of the gifts to the operation of the Spirit in giving spiritual gifts within the context of the body of believers. The greater amount of Paul's attention is given to the operation of the Spirit in the body. He dedicates two-thirds of chapter 12 and all of chapters 13 and 14 to the Spirit's operation in the body.

Operation of Gifts

In other texts, Paul used the principles of the primacy of the gift giver and the manifestations of the Spirit in the context of the church. One particular text is Ephesians 5:18-21. Luke also described these same principles in his description of Pentecost in Acts 2.

Control of the Spirit. The control of the gift giver was Paul's theme in Ephesians 5. He had already said, "Grieve not the holy Spirit" (4:30). Now he used the idea of being "filled" to emphasize the control of the gift giver: "And be not drunk with wine, wherein is excess; but be filled with the Spirit; Speaking to yourselves in psalms and hymns and spiritual songs, singing and making melody in your heart to the Lord; giving thanks always for all things unto God and the Father in the name of our Lord Jesus Christ; submitting yourselves one to another in the fear of God" (Ephesians 5:18-21).

The contrasting terms are *drunk* and *filled.* Just as a drunk person is under the influence of alcohol, the Spirit-filled believer is controlled by the Spirit.

What dominates your life? What is the center of your life? What is your life being spent for? What guides your life more than anything else? What do you care about more than anything else? These are questions Paul addressed when he exhorted, "Be filled with the Spirit."

After the exhortation, five descriptions of the Spirit-controlled life are given. The first four emphasize worship. "Speaking to yourselves in psalms and hymns and spiritual songs, singing and making melody in your heart to the Lord" emphasize both corporate and personal worship. A person rejoices and, in a very personal way, has a private time of worship and devotion unto the Lord. This happens as the person is individually concentrating upon the Lord, either when alone or in a worship service.

"Giving thanks . . . unto God" summarizes the basic expression of worship to God. The thanksgiving expressed is indicative of the believer's coming before God with thanksgiving just as the Old Testament saint came to God with an offering at the tabernacle.

"Submitting yourselves one to another in the fear of God" emphasizes the corporate context in which the Spirit manifests Himself. Love and unity were the contexts in which the Spirit came in Acts 2. Relationships and love for each other constitute Paul's greatest emphasis in 1 Corinthians 12—14.

"Submitting" indicates proper recognition and mutual relatedness to others in the body of Christ. "One to another" refers to submission of believers on a personal level and not just because of the rank or position of another. "In the fear of God" expresses the control and motivation for submitting. The motivation is neither the other person's position nor his personal merits. Submitting is rather an obedient response to the command of God. Submission is also an act of faith and devotion to God, not a romantic philosophy regarding the brotherhood of all people.

Paul pointed to God as the controller and the center of our focus, just as in 1 Corinthians 12 He is portrayed as the gift giver, the source. The context of the body of believers was also emphasized by Paul in his climactic exhortation to submit one to another.

Manifestation of the Spirit. The context of the body was one of the earliest emphases of Luke in describing Pentecost. He said they were "with one accord."

"And when the day of Pentecost was fully come, they were all with one accord in one place. And suddenly there came a sound from heaven as of a rushing mighty wind, and it filled all the house where they were sitting. And there appeared unto them cloven tongues like as of fire, and it sat upon each of them. And they were all filled with the Holy Ghost, and began to speak with other tongues, as the Spirit gave them utterance. And there were dwelling at Jerusalem Jews, devout men, out of every nation under heaven. Now when this was noised abroad, the multitude came together, and were confounded, because that every man heard them speak in his own language. And they were all amazed and marvelled, saying one to another, Behold, are not all these which speak Galileans? And how hear we every man in our own tongue, wherein we were born? . . . Cretes and Arabians, we do hear them speak in our tongues the wonderful works of God. And they were all amazed, and were in doubt, saying one to another, What meaneth this? Others mocking said, These men are full of new wine" (Acts 2:1-8; 11-13).

The Spirit of God resists divisiveness, is repulsed by disunity, and disdains rebellion. The loveliness of the Spirit is only welcomed by the beauty of the unity of the saints. "Accord" indicates unity of behavior—not that they all acted alike but that their behavior was consistent and complemented one another. They acted in harmony. Being part of the body of believers is prerequisite to being one with the Spirit (Ephesians 4:2-6).

God-centeredness is Luke's description of the believers in the Upper Room. That they were overwhelmed by God is his theme. An experience that came from God is his introduction and conclusion. In Acts 2:1-4, the wind coming from heaven begins the event and the conclusion is the utterance coming from the Spirit. Luke left no doubt in his readers' minds that the experience came from God.

The believers were first overwhelmed in their hearing when the mighty wind came upon them. Then their sight was overwhelmed when the flames sat upon them. Finally, they themselves were overwhelmed. Their personal overwhelming was marked by a specific occurrence—speaking in tongues unknown to them. The fact that speaking in other tongues is the initial evidence of baptism in the Holy Spirit was Luke's point, since he chose to exclude everything except this one feature of the personal overwhelming of the Spirit.

Tongues were not given to replace the proclamation of the gospel. The text says the people declared the wonderful works of God, which was the perfect prelude for Peter's preaching the gospel in his native tongue.

Luke provides insight into the manifestation of the Spirit by noting the crowd's observation. They thought the believers were drunk. The description of drunkenness is helpful in explaining the physical manifestations a person experiences when controlled by the Spirit. People under the Spirit's control may sway, pass out, stagger, dance, run, or exhibit other manifestations.

The Will of the Spirit. Returning to 1 Corinthians 12, we see that after listing the gifts in verses 8-10, Paul emphasized that the Spirit is the center and source of the gifts. His task was to stress the gift giver, not the content of the gift. Manifestations of the Spirit are by the Spirit to bring us into the Spirit.

"But all these worketh that one and the selfsame Spirit, dividing to every man severally as he will. For as the body is one, and hath many members, and all the members of that one body, being many, are one body; so also is Christ. For by one Spirit are we all baptized into one body, whether we be Jews or Gentiles, whether we be bond or free; and have been all made to drink into one Spirit" (vv. 11-13).

The work of the Spirit is determined by the Spirit. Neither the will of an individual nor the consensus of a group establish the Spirit's work. God himself sets the work of the Spirit within the body. Individually based manifestations and corporately generated activities are hollow and vain unless it is the Spirit who "worketh" among the members and is "dividing" (distributing) the gifts within the body of believers.

Unity in Diversity
1 Corinthians 12:14-31

The body of believers as the context in which the Spirit manifests Himself is a major theme in 1 Corinthians 12. Verses 14-27 emphasize the way in which the Spirit operates in the church.

Many Parts of the Same Body

"For the body is not one member, but many. If the foot shall say, Because I am not the hand, I am not of the body; is it therefore not of the body? And if the ear shall say, Because I am not the eye, I am not of the body; is it therefore not of the body?" (1 Corinthians 12:14-16).

No matter how powerfully the Spirit moves within a person, that person is still to be submissive to the body of believers. Being of the Spirit requires that we be of the body. No matter what the function, degree of uniqueness, or magnitude of the manifestation, the work of the Spirit will not draw a person away from the body. Instead, it will draw him closer to the body. This does not negate the corresponding responsibility of the body of believers to affirm each believer's individual gifts. The body's commitment to its members should enhance believers' commitment to the body.

Being of the body means recognizing other parts of the body of Christ and being submissive one to another. A person must be open to correction, willing to be taught, and able to take instruction from the body. The operation of the Spirit in a person's life is not inhibited by being knit with the people of the church, the structure of the church, or the authority within the church. On the contrary, failure to be part of the body distorts the Spirit's work in a person's life.

The local church at Corinth was part of the larger body of Christ with a central church in Jerusalem. The local body was accountable to the larger body of the church. A local church does not live unto itself. Just as members submit to the whole body in the operation of the Spirit, local bodies submit to organizational and denominational bodies and thereby facilitate the work of the Spirit.

One Body With Many Parts

"If the whole body were an eye, where were the hearing? If the whole were hearing, where were the smelling?" (1 Corinthians 12:17).

Member is not synonymous with *clone*. The church must seek the move of the Spirit distinctively and uniquely in lives. The Spirit will not operate exactly the same in each person's life. Not all functions within the church are duplicate. To be part of the body is to be used of the Spirit in a distinctive way.

God's Action Is the Key

"But now hath God set the members every one of them in the body, as it hath pleased him. And if they were all one member, where were the body? But now are they many members, yet but one body" (1 Corinthians 12:18-20).

What marks the balance between the member and the body of believers? What determines when and in what way the member affirms the body and when and how the body affirms individual members? The answer is the action of God. God set each member in the body. This is not a onetime action. God continually, according to what "hath pleased him," brings the members and the body into effective relationship.

Set (placed, arranged) in the Greek text emphasizes the definiteness of God's action. What occurs in the church in the operation of the Spirit should be understood as being set by the Lord. The work of the Spirit is not casually or haphazardly moved and changed by the whims of individuals or the pressure of groups. The functioning of the church, the very existence of the church, is established by God himself. An awesome humility must permeate the local body as it moves within what God has set in the church.

Program orientation, goal effectiveness, or human development do not determine the extent or manner in which the Spirit affirms both the body and individual members. Dysfunction between the body and its members reveals a lack of dependency on the action of God. Profound devotion to the God who operates in the manifestations of the Spirit is the key. Since programs, goals, and development do not create devotion, they must stem from consecration.

Care Rather Than Schism

"And the eye cannot say unto the hand, I have no need of thee: nor again the head to the feet, I have no need of you. Nay, much more those members of the body, which seem to be more feeble, are necessary: and those members of the body, which we think to be less honourable, upon these we bestow more abundant honour; and our uncomely parts have more abundant comeliness. For our comely parts have no need: but God hath tempered the body together, having given more abundant honour to that part which lacked: that there should be no schism in the body; but that the members should have the same care one for another. And whether one member suffer, all the members suffer with it; or one member be honoured, all the members rejoice with it" (1 Corinthians 12:21-26).

Care is God's creative action that brings the body and its members into effective relationship. The operation of the Spirit does not bypass the gifts of the Spirit. The gifts enhance the ability of the body to care. This principle is so important that Paul dealt more with care than with gifts.

Care stands at the pivot of Paul's teaching in chapter 12 on the operation of the Spirit. Leading up to the theme of care are the topics of need, feebleness, necessity, honor, comeliness, and schisms. Flowing from the theme of care are the topics of suffering, honor, and rejoicing. Verses 28-31 describe the gifts and offices the Spirit gives to a caring body.

A caring body makes each individual member feel a part of the *whole*. Rather than being fragmented, the group is unified. Individuals in the group mutually depend on and submit to one another. Just as the parts of a physical body work in coordination and depend upon one another, the individuals who make up a local body function with one another.

Schism is the opposite of care. Schism comes from the Greek term *schismas*, which means a tear, such as a tear in fabric. The implication is that force is exerted to separate elements of the fabric and the fabric is torn. Divisiveness is the sin that forces a tear in the fabric of the church, grieving the church and creating a break from one another and from God.

Just as an individual believer does not function in rebellion apart from the local body, neither does a local body function as an end unto itself. The beauty of a local congregation being established in relation to a larger church body is that it mirrors the Corinth-Jerusalem relationship. The schism of a local body from a central body encourages the schism of local believers from the local body.

The Individuality of Gifts

"And God hath set some in the church, first apostles, secondarily prophets, thirdly teachers, after that miracles, then gifts of healings, helps, governments, diversities of tongues. Are all apostles? are all prophets? are all teachers? are all workers of miracles? Have all the gifts of healing? do all speak with tongues? do all interpret? But covet earnestly the best gifts: and yet shew I unto you a more excellent way" (1 Corinthians 12:28-31).

Set was used again by Paul to stress the definiteness of God's action. The gifts and offices of the church have been established personally by God. He is the source and center of gifts and offices. The church functions with divine empowerment and establishing through gifts and offices. Far from business principles or motivational self-empowerment, offices and gifts are first of all God's agenda, set by Him.

More gifts and manifestations of the Spirit are given in verses 28-31. Some of them were already mentioned in verses 8-10; others are new. Paul was not giving an all-inclusive list that would never change.

The main point is the origin of the gifts—God. The content of the gift may vary, depending upon the will of God. Those traditional offices in the church (such as apostles and prophets) are names of the roles and functions in which particular gifts operate. Further, each office is to be filled by someone who feels God has gifted him for that office.

Does everyone have the same gifts? No, different gifts are given to different individuals. Paul preserved the individuality of gifts. Care of each member for one another is the theme of verses 21-27. The corresponding care of the body to preserve the distinctiveness of each member's giftedness is the theme of verses 28-31.

The local body of believers must be careful to affirm the individual giftedness of each believer. Guidance or even confrontation may be necessary, but the overall theme of the relationship of the local church to each member must be care. Giftedness is a powerful aspect of what God gives to believers. The local church must enhance that relationship and not become arrogant in it.

Correspondingly the local body must foster care between itself and the larger body, such as a denomination, represented by the Corinth-Jerusalem relationship, and the larger church must demonstrate care toward each local body of believers. God set the order of the early church, including the local church at Corinth and the leadership position of the church at Jerusalem. The tone of submission and leadership was caring one for another.

Paul used the expressions "best gifts" and "more excellent way" at the end of chapter 12. Some gifts are needed at certain times more than others; hence they are best for certain applications. However, regardless of the content of the gift, there is a principle that supersedes the best gifts—love. Paul set the context for this quality when he talked about care and the body.

The application of every gift must be tempered by love. Paul said love is so preeminent that the power of even the best gifts is lost when love is absent.

The Priority of Relationships and Love in the Body
1 Corinthians 13

Preeminence Over Self-centeredness

"Though I speak with the tongues of men and of angels, and have not charity, I am become as sounding brass, or a tinkling cymbal. And though I have the gift of prophecy, and understand all mysteries, and all knowledge; and though I have all faith, so that I could remove mountains, and have not charity, I am nothing. And though I bestow all my goods to feed the poor, and though I give my body to be burned, and have not charity, it profiteth me nothing" (1 Corinthians 13:1-3).

With resounding clarity and power, Paul expanded the relationship of love and spirituality to eternal proportions. He said spirituality is nothing without love. If a member of the body of Christ, though gifted by God, does not submit to and love the other members of the body, his spirituality is worthless and his effectiveness is lost.

Verses 1-3 apply this principle in contrast to the temptation of self-centeredness. These verses speak about an individual's great ability. The phrase "though I . . ." refers to personal skills and accomplishments. But no matter how great an individual's spiritual gifts are, without love and submission to others in the body, he is nothing in the eyes of God.

Preeminence Over Personal Struggle

"Charity suffereth long, and is kind; charity envieth not; charity vaunteth not itself, is not puffed up, doth not behave itself unseemly, seeketh not her own, is not easily provoked, thinketh no evil" (1 Corinthians 13:4, 5).

No matter how tempted one may be to give in to impatience, irrititability, short-temperedness, and unkindness, the display of these actions is not love. No matter how unlovable a fellow Christian may be, love demonstrates a generous and gentle spirit, a magnanimity of mind and action. Because God has been gracious to us is reason enough to keep us from spiritual pride and to prod us toward right actions in all our relationships.

Preeminence Over Surroundings

"Rejoiceth not in iniquity, but rejoiceth in the truth; beareth all things, believeth all things, hopeth all things, endureth all things" (1 Corinthians 13:6, 7).

Love takes no pleasure in the moral failure of others. An individual who rejoices in the downfall of another is not the possessor of love toward that person.

Preeminence Through Perfection

"Charity never faileth: but whether there be prophecies, they shall fail; whether there be tongues, they shall cease; whether there be knowledge, it shall vanish away. For we know in part, and we prophesy in part. But when that which is perfect is come, then that which is in part shall be done away" (1 Corinthians 13:8-10).

Love, submission, and unity are preeminent over giftedness, personal struggle, and circumstances because love is at the heart of the perfection of God. Love endures even when other functions of the believer and the church are fulfilled and eclipsed by God's perfect plan.

Perfect refers to the work of God. That work always maintains love and reconciliation at its core. God in eternity loved man and sent the Redeemer to him. That love will never fail throughout eternity. Unfailing spirituality is only produced as it abides within the context of unfailing love for fellow believers.

Preeminence in Progress

"When I was a child, I spake as a child, I understood as a child, I thought as a child: but when I became a man, I put away childish things. For now we see through a glass, darkly; but then face to face: now I know in part; but then shall I know even as also I am known" (1 Corinthians 13:11, 12).

Paul clarified that the perfection of love is an ongoing process. The full perfecting of God's work has not yet occurred. Just as a child grows, so does the love of God multiply among the saints. The eventual picture of God's love in the life of the church is but dimly seen and only later will it be fully clear.

The pivotal point of Paul's description of the process of love is the phrase "face to face." The perfection of God's love will be known when the Lord is seen face-to-face. The fulfillment and perfection of our love will be based upon our relationship with Him.

Preeminence in the Present

"And now abideth faith, hope, charity, these three; but the greatest of these is charity" (1 Corinthians 13:13).

Paul's concluding appeal was to the current reality of love. While the full perfection of God's love will be known in our future relationship with Him, this did not diminish the current reality of love. Love for God and others, especially those of the household of faith, is something that "abideth."

Not only did Paul stress the reality of love in the present, but he also emphasized the priority of love. More than any other factor, love determines the worth of our spiritual effectiveness. Paul began chapter 13 emphasizing this priority, and he concluded the passage in the same way. God will bless His people in no greater measure than their love for one another. Spiritual power is measured by brotherly love.

The Personal Dimension of the Operation of the Spirit

1 Corinthians 14:1-11

Paul moved from exposition in 1 Corinthians 12 and exhortation in chapter 13 to instruction in chapter 14. Personal spirituality and corporate sensitivity are applied to the local church setting. Paul had been teaching on two themes—the operation of the Spirit within the individual and within the body of believers as the context within which the Spirit operates.

These two principles are discussed once more as they apply to personal devotions and corporate worship services.

The Purpose of Tongues and Prophesying

"Follow after charity, and desire spiritual gifts, but rather that ye may prophesy. For he that speaketh in an unknown tongue speaketh not unto men, but unto God: for no man understandeth him; howbeit in the spirit he speaketh mysteries. But he that prophesieth speaketh unto men to edification, and exhortation, and comfort. He that speaketh in an unknown tongue edifieth himself; but he that prophesieth edifieth the church. I would that ye all spake with tongues, but rather that ye prophesied: for greater is he that prophesieth than he that speaketh with tongues, except he interpret, that the church may receive edifying" (1 Corinthians 14:1-5).

In chapter 14 Paul used tongues and prophesying as expressions to communicate the two themes he used throughout chapters 12 and 13—the personal and corporate dimension of the operation of the Spirit. Speaking in tongues, along with spiritual gifts, is the expression for the personal dimension. Prophesying is the major expression for the corporate dimension.

Speaking in tongues is used by the Spirit in our personal times of devotion. A person may speak in tongues in a corporate context, but without interpretation the benefit is still primarily personal. The communication is known only to God. The words are "mysteries" (v. 2) to men. Paul was not speaking of foreign languages, or of speech known to the speaker but rather of speech unknown to the speaker or any other person in the congregation.

"But rather that ye may prophesy" (v. 1) and "greater is he that prophesieth" (v. 5) emphasize the importance of the corporate dimension. When the body is gathered together, the Spirit-filled believer must be sensitive to the corporate dimension.

Rather and *greater* do not indicate any superiority of prophesying or the corporate operation of the Spirit over tongues, gifts, or any personal manifestation of the Spirit. Paul expressed his desire that all would experience tongues and be desirous of spiritual gifts (vv. 1, 5). He commanded the Corinthians not to forbid members to speak in tongues (v. 39).

Paul wanted to be certain the corporate dimension was emphasized when the body was gathered together, but he did not minimize the personal dimension. His emphasis was that when the body is gathered together, it benefits more from prophesying—a corporate dimension of the Spirit's operation.

Paul gave a threefold definition of *prophesying* in verse 3: edification, exhortation, and comfort. *Edification* means to build up. *Exhortation,* in this context, means to come alongside of another. *Comfort* means to bring cheer.

Some believe prophesying meant preaching, but there is no mention of preaching in this passage. The emphasis is upon the threefold purpose of building up one another, becoming closer together, and encouraging one another. Benefit to the body so that all may have understanding was Paul's emphasis.

Tongues and Being Understood

"Now, brethren, if I come unto you speaking with tongues, what shall I profit you, except I shall speak to you either by revelation, or by knowledge, or by prophesying, or by doctrine? And even things without life giving sound, whether pipe or harp, except they give a distinction in the sounds, how shall it be known what is piped or harped? For if the trumpet give an uncertain sound, who shall prepare himself to the battle? So likewise ye, except ye utter by the tongue words easy to be understood, how shall it be known what is spoken? for ye shall speak into the air. There are, it may be, so many kinds of voices in the world, and none of them is without signification. Therefore if I know not the meaning of the voice, I shall be unto him that speaketh a barbarian, and he that speaketh shall be a barbarian unto me" (1 Corinthians 14:6-11).

Benefit to the body is Paul's concern. Though an individual may benefit from the Spirit, that person must also be concerned about the benefit to the body as a whole. The sensitivity of Paul must be the sensitivity of the Pentecostal believer today. Receiving a blessing is not the only goal of Pentecost. The ultimate goal is that all of us, individually and corporately, will be blessed.

The body receives "profit" (benefit and advantage) when manifestations of the Spirit are given with understanding (v. 6). The manifestations Paul listed include revelation, knowledge, prophesying, and doctrine. Each has a certain emphasis, but their common goal is to profit the body.

Revelation is the giving of divine insight, emphasizing discernment and perspective. *Knowledge* is the giving of information through divine means, emphasizing the content of what is given. *Prophesying* is a word giving insight into current or future events, emphasizing that the message is indeed from God. *Doctrine* is a teaching for the church, emphasizing the instructive nature of the information.

Ignorance of what God is doing results if we are self-focused Pentecostals. We are as barbarians and fools to one another if we gather together insensitive to the corporate dimension of the Spirit. Chaos is the result. The rumble of an orchestra out of tune is our sound. What we may not realize is that sensitivity to the Spirit includes our sensitivity to one another.

This in no way detracts from the personal dimension of the Spirit's operation. Paul sought to revive in the Corinthians a devout sensitivity to their brothers and sisters. The Spirit calls us not only to be responsible for our spirituality but also to make an investment in the spirituality of our fellow Christians.

The Operation of the Spirit Is for the Body
1 Corinthians 14:12-40

Edification of the Church

"Even so ye, forasmuch as ye are zealous of spiritual gifts, seek that ye may excel to the edifying of the church" (1 Corinthians 14:12).

The zeal for a move of the Spirit in one's life should be matched by a desire to excel in the corporate dimension. *Zealous* comes from the Greek term *zelotes*, which in its root form means to boil. Excel (Greek, *perisseuo*) emphasizes completeness or abounding. What gives the exhortation of verse 12 power is its relationship to zeal and excellence. We should be just as zealous, if not more so, to excel in attaining excellence in the spirituality of the body as a whole as we are zealous to excel in the personal dimension spiritually. "Even so," "forasmuch," and "that ye may" all point to the correlation of personal zeal excelling for the benefit of the church.

Edification Through Understood Speech

"Wherefore let him that speaketh in an unknown tongue pray that he may interpret. For if I pray in an unknown tongue, my spirit prayeth, but my understanding is unfruitful. What is it then? I will pray with the spirit, and I will pray with the understanding also: I will sing with the spirit, and I will sing with the understanding also. Else when thou shalt bless with the spirit, how shall he that occupieth the room of the unlearned say Amen at thy giving of thanks, seeing he understandeth not what thou sayest? For thou verily givest thanks well, but the other is not edified" (1 Corinthians 14:13-17).

How do you channel personal zeal into corporate excellence? Pray that the operation of the Spirit will be for the corporate good. Tongues are useful for the corporate body when they are interpreted. Whatever blessing comes from the Spirit to individuals, may it be a blessing to the body also.

Prayer is the key to edification. Fully dependent upon the work of the Spirit, we pray that the Spirit, by His will, may operate through us for the good of our brothers and sisters.

Understanding is our responsibility. We do not

remain completely passive. It is clearly revealed in this passage that the Spirit's will is for the body to be edified by the power of the Spirit. We must be obedient to the Spirit and pray, sing, bless, give thanks, and allow the Spirit to move within us in such a way that we respond with understandable speech. Paul said the Spirit also operates in understood speech and we must yield to the Spirit in understood speech when we gather as a body.

Edify comes from the same root as the word for building a house or structure. Fellow believers need to be built up, allowing the construction of Christlikeness within them. The will of the Spirit is that they be built up. Resisting the Spirit's call to edify through understood language is a failure to be used by God for the benefit of others.

Understanding and Edification

"I thank my God, I speak with tongues more than ye all: yet in the church I had rather speak five words with my understanding, that by my voice I might teach others also, than ten thousand words in an unknown tongue. Brethren, be not children in understanding: howbeit in malice be ye children, but in understanding be men" (1 Corinthians 14:18-20).

Commitment to others and a desire to see God work in others must be as strong as our desire for personal blessing when we gather together as a Spirit-filled church. Paul strongly set forth the priority of corporate blessing. Ten thousand words of unknown speech, though from the Spirit, may not have the value of five words of understood speech by the Spirit. Unknown speech edifies the speaker, but understood speech edifies others in a congregational worship setting.

A faith commitment is at the root of Paul's commitment to the work of the Spirit in the lives of others. When setting forth the priority of others, he said, "I thank my God" (v. 18). Refusal to seek blessing for others is a statement about our walk with God and not just our opinion of others. When we gather as Pentecostals, our first prayer must be "Holy Spirit, use me for others."

Tongues and Individual Understanding

"In the law it is written, With men of other tongues and other lips will I speak unto this people; and yet for all that will they not hear me, saith the Lord. Wherefore tongues are for a sign, not to them that believe, but to them that believe not: but prophesying serveth not for them that believe not, but for them which believe. If therefore the whole church be come together into one place, and all speak with tongues, and there come in those that are unlearned, or unbelievers, will they not say that ye are mad? But if all prophesy, and there come in one that believeth not, or one unlearned, he is convinced of all, he is judged of all: and thus are the secrets of his heart made manifest; and so falling down on his face he will worship God, and report that God is in you of a truth" (1 Corinthians 14:21-25).

For the individual, tongues serve as a sign but remain incomplete without prophesying or interpretation. Paul quoted Isaiah 28:11, 12, a passage which foretold that God would use unknown tongues to speak to individuals. However, the purpose is to present a sign—a pointer, a marker. A sign gives direction. It points the way, but the message and substance of the destination are not fully indicated. Though tongues serve a necessary purpose, understandable speech is required for the full work of God to be revealed.

Prophesying is the term used for understood speech from God. Joel 2:28 refers to prophesying and Peter referred to prophesying twice in his message at Pentecost (Acts 2:17-18). Through unknown speech, the Spirit puts a person in direct communication with God (1 Corinthians 14:2). Having been in communion with God, the Spirit-filled believer then can speak as one who has been with God.

The model for prophesying is the prophets of old. They spoke as "thus saith the Lord." They had been with God. God had spoken to them. Their message was not the message of men but of God. Paul was not concerned with mere language. He used "prophesy" because he was speaking of speech from one who had been in communion with God. Prophesying is understood speech that grows out of communion with God when we have fellowship with Him by the Spirit.

Prophesying probes the heart (v. 25), not just the mind. Paul was concerned with more than understanding. He addressed understandable speech that penetrates the spirit of others. The goal is not mere comprehension but to have others worship God.

Tongues and Corporate Understanding

"How is it then, brethren? when ye come together, every one of you hath a psalm, hath a doctrine, hath a tongue, hath a revelation, hath an interpretation. Let all things be done unto edifying. If any man speak in an unknown tongue, let it be by two, or at the most by three, and that by course; and let one interpret. But if there be no interpreter, let him keep silence in the church; and let him speak to himself, and to God. Let the prophets speak two or three, and let the other judge. If any thing be revealed to another that sitteth by, let the first hold his peace. For ye may all prophesy one by one, that all may learn, and all may be comforted" (1 Corinthians 14:26-31).

Tongues in the corporate setting must be monitored by the body. Though unknown speech is for private benefit, in the context of the body of believers the effectiveness of unknown tongues is the responsibility of the body. Paul described the process by which the body functions to make the use of unknown tongues effective for the body as a whole.

Three guidelines are given for the use of unknown tongues in corporate worship: (1) They are to be given in order, or "by course" (Greek, *ana meros*), meaning in turn or one at a time. (2) The number of those speaking to the body in an unknown tongue is to be limited. (3) Interpretation is to be sought from God so that the sense of the Spirit's operation is known.

Paul stated these guidelines and then repeated them in reverse fashion. He said if there is no interpreter, the person speaking in an unknown tongue should speak for his personal edification in a manner that does not affect the rest of the body during the service. This in no way eliminates tongues during church when there is not an interpretation. A person can speak in an unknown tongue during a service for personal edification and not be a hindrance to others. What volume is appropriate cannot be easily answered, but speaking in tongues for personal edification during a worship service does not necessarily mean a disruption of what God is doing in the lives of others.

No more than two or three are to be used in prophesying (v. 29), and the others should be able to discern the prophecy for effective ministry to the body. If the Spirit is using someone else, another individual should remain silent (v. 30) until it is his turn (v. 27).

Tongues and Authority (Origin)

"And the spirits of the prophets are subject to the prophets. For God is not the author of confusion, but of peace, as in all churches of the saints. Let your women keep silence in the churches: for it is not permitted unto them to speak; but they are commanded to be under obedience, as also saith the law. And if they will learn any thing, let them ask their husbands at home: for it is a shame for women to speak in the church. What? came the word of God out from you? or came it unto you only? If any man think himself to be a prophet, or spiritual, let him acknowledge that the things that I write unto you are the commandments of the Lord. But if any man be ignorant, let him be ignorant" (1 Corinthians 14:32-38).

Effectiveness for ministry is dependent upon our yielding to the authority of the Spirit. This passage emphasizes orderliness. Individually and corporately, God expects believers to be used by the Spirit.

However, He does not expect them to allow their own spirit to violate the Holy Spirit's parameters of order and thus cause confusion. The Spirit will not violate an individual, the family, or the body. The means by which these lines of integrity maintain the genuine effectiveness of the Spirit's work is His authority.

God has "set" (12:28) the order of the church's offices. The authority behind the operation of the gifts and offices is God. The offices and gifts are not subject to human whim. Individuals merely receive, participate, and subject themselves under the authority of the Spirit. God has set the order and arrangement of the operation of His Spirit in the church. Offices and structures are set by God for the purpose of enhancing the operation of His Spirit.

The individual participates in the authority structure by subjecting his spirit as he responds to the Spirit of God. The Spirit edifies the body as a whole. An individual must subject himself, or control his spirit's responses, to the Holy Spirit so as to edify others.

Purpose, direction, and effectiveness are the earmarks of order. The body exercises authority by maintaining order and avoiding confusion. The process of order is similar to what Paul meant when he instructed that manifestations of tongues to the body (not tongues for personal use during a service) be done one at a time in order (14:27). Disunity, self-centeredness, and vanity are the marks of confusion. The result is ineffectiveness.

The authority of the Lord is communicated by His commandments. The Word of God—"commandments of the Lord" (v. 37)—is the standard by which the operation of the Spirit is understood. The believer must ultimately subject all that he does to the Word. Paul's message is that he was writing with an appeal to the standard of the Word. Neither individuals nor the body of believers operate under their own jurisdiction. The move of the Spirit on both the individual and corporate levels is guided by the will of the Lord as revealed by His Word. Claiming any less is to fall prey to chaos or uncontrolled use of the operation of the Spirit.

The family system of authority was also part of Paul's instruction. Women were not the problem in verses 34 and 35—confusion was. The text does not imply that women, because they are women, are used any less by the Spirit. Paul had already recognized the authority of women to prophesy (11:5). Nevertheless, lack of order within the body of the church was hindering the effective ministry of the Spirit.

Verses 36 and 37 summarize Paul's emphasis upon authority. Paul covered three levels of authority: God's authority, the authority of the body, and the authority of the individual over his own spirit. The first level of authority is the Word of God, coming from God and reflecting His authority. The second level is in the body of believers. The authority to be a prophet comes from God and reflects the function of a person to benefit the gathered church within the authority of the body. The third level concerns the individual's control of his own spirit. The means to be spiritual comes from God and reflects the individual's authority over his own spirit's response to the Holy Spirit's action. Though these three are all levels of authority that affect the operation of the Spirit, the guiding and superseding authority is that of God's Word—the commandments of the Lord.

Affirming the Personal and Corporate Dimensions of the Operation of the Spirit

"Wherefore, brethren, covet to prophesy, and forbid not to speak with tongues. Let all things be done decently and in order" (1 Corinthians 14:39, 40).

Tongues have not ceased, and the church still has authority in spiritual matters. Evidently, in Paul's day there were individuals who reflected one of two extremes. Either they wanted to do away with the individual experience of the Spirit reflected in unknown tongues or they wanted to be used in speaking in tongues anytime or anywhere, even if others were not edified by the speaking.

"Wherefore" extends the idea of commandment from verses 37 and 38. Paul's instruction about the personal and corporate dimensions (forbid not the personal and foster the corporate) are commandments from the Lord.

"Decently and in order" in verse 40 captures both the personal and corporate dimensions of the Spirit's operation. *Decently* indicates that which is becoming and enriching to the individual. *Order* emphasizes the manner of the Spirit that edifies others in a fellowship.

Being used of the Spirit to speak in tongues for individual edification is a blessed experience to be fostered and not forbidden privately or while in a church service. The desire of the Spirit-filled believer should be to edify others through speech that is understood. The characteristic which identifies that God is truly operating in individuals and the corporate body is that both dimensions are affirmed and neither is excluded.

The Holy Spirit
in Church
History

5

Dr. Robert White is general overseer of the Church of God.

Dr. White has served the church in many administrative positions, including assistant general overseer, World Missions director, Executive Council member, School of Theology president, director of the General Department of Education, state overseer, and state youth and Christian education director.

Robert White

he Pentecostal revival began inauspiciously in the closing years of the 19th century and the opening years of this century. From humble beginnings the Pentecostal Movement has grown into a globe-circling religious force. Today more than 400 million people around the world profess the Holy Spirit baptism.

Though the scope of the modern Pentecostal Movement has no parallel in Christian history, outpourings of the Spirit have continued throughout church history. While most opponents of speaking in tongues admit that tongues were in evidence in the New Testament church, they are quick to assert that Holy Spirit baptism evidenced by speaking in other tongues ended a few years after the Day of Pentecost. However, religious history paints an entirely different portrait of the Holy Spirit's presence in the church. There is absolutely no doubt that the outpouring of the Holy Spirit which began on the Day of Pentecost continued throughout church history to this very day and has been accompanied by speaking in tongues as the Spirit gives the utterance.

Endued With Power

The present-day outpouring of the Holy Spirit is more than a 20th-century religious phenomenon. It has roots in the earliest history of the church. In fact, the initial outpouring of the Spirit on the Day of Pentecost heralded the opening of the New Testament church age.

Before Jesus ascended to heaven, He gave His disciples both a promise and a commandment: "And, behold, I send the promise of my Father upon you: but tarry ye in the city of Jerusalem, until ye be endued with power from on high" (Luke 24:49).

Jesus assured the disciples He would send them the promise of His Father. However, before they could receive the promise, they must keep His commandment to tarry in Jerusalem until they were endued with power from on high.

Luke repeated Jesus' command to the disciples in Acts 1:4, 5: "And, being assembled together with them, commanded them that they should not depart from Jersusalem, but wait for the promise of the Father, which, saith he, ye have heard of me. For John truly baptized with water; but ye shall be baptized with the Holy Ghost not many days hence."

This enduement with power was to enable them to be witnesses of Him. Jesus told the disciples: "But ye shall receive power, after that the Holy Ghost is come upon you: and ye shall be witnesses unto me both in Jerusalem, and in all Judaea, and in Samaria, and unto the uttermost part of the earth" (Acts 1:8).

After Jesus' ascension from Mount Olivet, the disciples returned to Jerusalem and "went up into an upper room" (v. 13). There they "all continued with one accord in prayer and supplication with the women, and Mary the mother of Jesus, and with his brethren" (v. 14). Verse 15 records that the number of disciples was about 120.

For about 10 days the group prayed and waited. Then, on the day of the Feast of Pentecost, when devout Jews from many lands were gathered in Jerusalem, the eagerly awaited event transpired. Luke described that momentous occasion this way:

> And when the day of Pentecost was fully come, they were all with one accord in one place. And suddenly there came a sound from heaven as of a rushing mighty wind, and it filled all the house where they were sitting. And there appeared unto them cloven tongues like as of fire, and it sat upon each of them. And they were all filled with the Holy Ghost, and began to speak with other tongues, as the Spirit gave them utterance (Acts 2:1-4).

The outpouring prophesied by Joel (2:28, 29), the baptism of fire foretold by John the Baptist (Matthew 3:11), and the Comforter promised by Jesus (John 14:16) had come!

All the disciples were filled with the Spirit, and they *all* spoke with other tongues, as the Spirit gave them utterance (Acts 2:4). The outpouring of power foreshadowed in the Old Testament anointings of kings, priests, prophets, and other individuals called to a special work was now a reality for *all* God's people. No longer would the Spirit be received by only a select few. Young and old, men and women, master and servant, *all* could now call upon the name of the Lord and be filled with the Spirit.

Endued with power, the infant church went forth testifying of Jesus in the power of the Spirit. When Peter preached the first Pentecostal message, 3,000 souls came to the Lord (v. 41). The church "continued stedfastly in the apostles' doctrine and fellowship, and in breaking of bread, and in prayers. . . . And many wonders and signs were done by the apostles. . . . And the Lord added to the church daily such as should be saved" (vv. 42, 43, 47).

A man lame from birth was healed when Peter and John prayed for him (Acts 3). This provided the opportunity to preach Christ, and 5,000 people became believers (4:4).

Another outpouring of the Spirit is recorded in Acts 4. When the church prayed, the place where they were assembled was shaken "and they were all filled with the Holy Ghost, and they spake the word of God with boldness" (v. 31).

The most notable result of the enduement with power throughout the New Testament era was preaching Christ and winning people to the Lord (5:42). This is true in Pentecostal churches today. Spirit-filled believers know they are endued with power to proclaim the gospel of Christ, not simply to speak in tongues.

Early church leaders considered preaching so important that they appointed seven Spirit-filled men to administer the business of the church so that the apostles could give themselves "continually to prayer, and to the ministry of the word" (6:4). As a result, "the word of God increased; and the number of the disciples multiplied in Jerusalem greatly" (v. 7). Many of the Jewish priests were converted to Christianity, and great wonders and miracles were done among the people (vv. 7, 8).

The Pentecostal outpouring soon produced the first Christian martyr. As he was being stoned to death, Stephen, a man full of the Holy Spirit, looked into the heavens and saw Jesus at the right hand of God (7:54-58).

The persecution that arose following Stephen's martyrdom brought revival. A devout and zealous Jew, Saul led the attack on the church, making havoc of it and imprisoning believers. As the Christians fled persecution, they "went every where preaching the word" (8:4). Endued with power and on fire with Pentecostal fervor, Philip went to Samaria "and preached Christ unto them" (v. 5). A great revival that was evidenced by miracles, healings, deliverance from demons, and conversions broke out.

When news of the revival in Samaria reached the apostles, they sent Peter and John to investigate. When they arrived in Samaria, they prayed for the people to receive the Holy Spirit. "Then laid they their hands on them, and they received the Holy Ghost" (v. 17).

In Caesarea, Cornelius, a devout centurion was praying when he saw a vision of an angel. The angel instructed Cornelius to send to Joppa for Peter, who would tell him what he ought to do (10:1-6). Peter came to Cornelius' house and preached Christ. While Peter was preaching, the Spirit fell on all who heard the Word (v. 44).

The Jews who had accompanied Peter were astonished. To their surprise, God had also poured out the Holy Spirit upon Gentiles. How did they know? "They heard them speak with tongues, and magnify God" (v. 46). Based upon this evidence, Peter said they had "received the Holy Ghost as well as we" (v. 47).

In Acts 19, Paul (Saul), now converted and a preacher of the gospel, found certain disciples at Ephesus. He asked if they had received the Holy Spirit since they had believed (v. 2). When Paul learned that their instruction about baptism included only the baptism of John, he preached to them, baptized them in water, and then laid hands on them and prayed for them to be filled with the Spirit. The Spirit came upon them and they spoke with tongues (v. 6).

After the Ephesian baptism, no specific references are made to individuals receiving the baptism in the Holy Spirit. However, this in no way indicates a cessation of the experience. Instead, from that point on the historical narrative changes to the story of Paul's increasing opposition from the Jews, his arrest, and his journey to Rome.

But even then, the account is sprinkled with references to the Holy Spirit's presence in the church. Acts 20:28 refers to the Holy Spirit's making men overseers in the church. Acts 21:4, 11 mentions men prophesying by the Spirit.

Beginning with the Book of Romans, the emphasis is upon the Spirit's work in individual lives and in the church. In his letters to the Corinthian church, Paul gave instruction concerning the gifts of the Spirit and their proper operation in the church. The provision of regulations for the operation of spiritual gifts anticipates their continuation in the life of the church. The continuing references to the Holy Spirit show that the Holy Spirit baptism continued to be a vital part of the New Testament church beyond the events of the Book of Acts.

The Holy Spirit in Church History

The written record of church history documents the fact that the Holy Spirit baptism with the initial evidence of tongues-speaking never died out but has been in evidence throughout the history of the Christian church.

The Interpreter's Dictionary of the Bible states that "through the centuries glossolalia has frequently reappeared among Christian groups."[1]

G.B. Cutten, author of a 1927 work titled *Speaking With Tongues*, said: "Many isolated examples of speaking with tongues might be given, extending down through the ages. . . . In most cases the appearance of speaking with tongues has been connected with revival experiences."[2]

The *Twentieth Century Encyclopedia of Religious Knowledge* says: "The phenomenon of 'speaking with tongues as the Spirit gives utterance' (Acts 2:1-13) has appeared in all ages of the Church."[3]

In his *History of the Apostolic Church*, noted historian Philip Schaff said, "The speaking with tongues, however, was not confined to the Day of Pentecost. . . . This gift perpeturated itself. We find traces of it still in the second and third centuries."[4]

Harper's Bible Dictionary asserts:

That this phenomenon is by no means restricted to

early Christianity is universally recognized. It was common in the Christian movement as late as Tertullian and Irenaeus. By the time of Chrysostom it had apparently died out; at least the good bishop found difficulty in understanding what it really was. This, however, was but temporary. In later years it reappeared again, and has been the seemingly inevitable consequence of all extended seasons of "revivals."[5]

In a *Saturday Evening Post* article about the Charismatic renewal, McCandlish Phillips wrote, "Praying in tongues has recurred at intervals throughout the Christian era, although it did not affect large masses until early in this century."[6]

The *Encyclopaedia Britannica* declares that miraculous utterances recur in Christian revivals in every age.[7]

In the *Catholic Biblical Encyclopedia*, John E. Steinmueller and Kathryn Sullivan wrote, "In regard to the perpetuation of these charisms, it may be said that, although they were manifested more frequently in the infant Church and the first few centuries, they have never been completely lacking in the Church."[8] Later, in the same work, Steinmueller and Sullivan declared, "Glossolalia was a true charism of the Holy Spirit."[9]

F.L. Cross, writing in *The Oxford Dictionary of the Christian Church*, said, "Similar phenomena are constantly met with in religious revivals."[10]

Referring to these writings, R. Leonard Carroll said:

These references strike a death blow to the protracted assertion that tongues speaking had been filed away after the birth of the New Testament church. We are reminded that if these gifted writers can be trusted in one area of reporting, it follows that they can also be trusted when they discussed tongues speaking.[11]

Carroll also said:

If tongues speaking had not ceased to occur, what forces contributed to much of the silence on the subject? Evidence comes to us from Eusebius of Caesarea, the "father of church history," who lived from about A.D. 260 to 340. The Church History of Eusebius presents a low estimation of a certain sect of tongues speakers. This segment of historical data discloses far more, however, than the disrepute of a few disorderly people. It is highly significant that the record also reveals startling trends in religious interpretation and emphasis at this particular period of time. It is evident and noteworthy, however, that the sarcasm and ridicule focus directly upon the very fact that the glossolalia phenomenon was actually in operation.[12]

Carroll concluded:

Of no little significance is the fact that the rich enthusiasm and vocal testimony which marked the Early Church had almost disappeared by the middle of the second century. Yet, in the midst of an atmosphere that was not conducive to spiritual phenomena, tongues speaking continued![13]

Two second-century works, *The Didache* and *The Shepherd of Hermas*, confirm that people of that period spoke in tongues.

Irenaeus, the bishop of Lyons, was a student of Polycarp and lived about A.D. 115 to 202. Polycarp had direct contact with the apostle John, thus giving Irenaeus a direct link back to the apostles. In *Against Heresies*, Irenaeus wrote:

> For [God] promised, that in the last times He would pour Him [the Spirit] upon [His] servants and handmaids, that they might prophesy. . . . This Spirit . . . also, as Luke says, descended at the day of Pentecost upon the disciples after the Lord's ascension . . . from whence also, with one accord in all languages, they uttered praise to God.[14]

Concerning tongues speaking in his day, Irenaeus said:

> In like manner we do hear [or have heard] many brethren in the Church, who possess prophetic gifts, and who through the Spirit speak all kinds of languages, and bring to light for the general benefit the hidden things of men, and declare the mysteries of God, whom also the apostle terms "spiritual," they being spiritual because they partake of the Spirit.[15]

Elaborating on Irenaeus' statement, Carroll wrote:

> A careful reading of the reference extracts the thorn of critics and should silence them forever. There is no speculation in the report. The tongues speaking was actually heard. Brethren spoke all kinds of languages through the anointing of the Holy Ghost. . . . 'Many brethren' denotes that the miracle of tongues was not relegated to a few outcasts. They were warmly listed as 'brethren' not brawlers. The occasion centered within the confines of the living

church. Perhaps it was alarming to some people that the operation of the glossolalia phenomenon was not an isolated occurrence. The stage for tongues speaking was the church, not a dark alley. The miracle of utterance was not an aimless occurrence. It was to declare the mysteries of God and to reveal hidden things of men for the general benefit of all concerned. In the final analysis, the hallmark of the tongues speakers was that they were spiritual people.[16]

Tertullian (150-222), a North African who is often called the dean of Western Christianity, defended speaking in tongues when he wrote:

Now all these signs (of spiritual gifts) are forthcoming from my side without any difficulty; and they agree, too, with the rules, and the dispensations, and the instructions of the Creator; therefore without doubt the Christ, and the Spirit, and the Apostle, belong severally to my God. Here, then, is my frank avowal for any one who cares to require it.[17]

Pachomius, an Egyptian monk, "after seasons of prayer, under the power of the Spirit, was able to speak languages which he had never learned."[18] Philip Schaff said, "Tradition ascribes to him all sorts of miracles, even the gift of tongues."[19]

Christian philosopher Origen defended tongues speaking by Christian prophets when they were ridiculed by Celsus, who said: "To these promises are added strange, fanatical, and quite unintelligible words, of which no rational person can find the meaning."[20] Both the attack and Origen's defense of the tongues-speakers prove the Holy Spirit baptism with the evidence of tongues was still occurring in Origen's day.

The writings of Gregory Nazianzen, Basil, Hilary of Potiers, Ambrose, and Leo all testify to the presence of the Holy Spirit in church history.

The *Encyclopaedia Britannica* states that speaking in tongues occurred "among the mendicant friars of the 13th century."[21]

Vincent Ferrer, Spanish preacher and missionary who died in 1419, won thousands of people to the Lord in Spain, Italy, and France. Philip Schaff wrote of Ferrer:

> Able to speak only Spanish, his sermons, though they were not interpreted, are reported to have been understood in France and Italy. The gift of tongues was ascribed to him by his contemporaries as well as the gift of miracles.[22]

Bridget, the daughter of Swedish prince Birger, is reported to have been able "to speak the language of angels."[23]

Alban Butler wrote of Lewis Bertrand, who was born in Spain in 1526, "The gift of tongues, of prophecy, and of miracles, were favors conferred by heaven on this new apostle, as the authentic history of his life . . . assures us."[24]

Butler also wrote of Camillus De Lellis, born in Italy in 1550, "God testified his approbation of the saint's zeal by the spirit of prophecy and the gift of miracles, on several occasions, and by many heavenly communications."[25]

Martin Luther, the great reformer, was said to have been "a prophet, evangelist, speaker in tongues and interpreter, in one person, endowed with all the gifts of the Holy Spirit."[26]

Calvin, the leader of French Protestantism, wrote concerning tongues:

At present great theologians . . . disclaim against them with furious zeal. As it is certain, that the Holy Spirit has here honoured the use of tongues with never-dying praise, we may very readily gather, what is the kind of spirit that actuates these reformers, who level as many reproaches as they can against the pursuit of them.

. . . Paul, nevertheless, commends the use of tongues. So far is he from wishing them abolished or thrown away.[27]

In the mid-1500s, severe persecution arose against Protestants in France. Many sought refuge in the mountains of Cevennes. There "the spiritual gifts of the Apostolic Church reappeared—miracles of healing, prophecy, and talking with tongues."[28]

Concerning the French Huguenots, Bruey wrote:

The most striking instances of the gift of tongues in modern times are 'the little prophets of Cevennes' at the close of the seventeenth century and the Irvingites early in the nineteenth; and it is remarkable that these exhibited respectively the phenomenon of the Day of Pentecost as portrayed in the Book of Acts and the ecstasies which convulsed the Corinthian Church. . . . They preached and exhorted, not in the Romance patois of their native mountains, but in good French.[29]

John Wesley, the founder of Methodism, whose life spanned most of the 1800s, said in a letter to a friend:

> I must observe an historical mistake which occurs toward the bottom of your next page. Since the Reformation, you say: "This gift [tongues] has never once been heard of, or pretended to, by the Romanist themselves." (Page 122.) But has it been pretended to (whether justly or not) by no others, though not by the Romanists? Has it "never once been heard of" since that time? Sir, your memory fails you again. . . . It has been heard of more than once, no farther off than the valleys of Dauphiny [France].[30]

These accounts taken from varied periods of church history show a continuing experience of Holy Spirit baptism across the centuries. It is certain that many other people also were baptised in the Holy Spirit and spoke in tongues without the account of their experience being recorded. These Spirit-filled believers were the forerunners of the spiritual awakening that would eventually birth the modern Pentecostal Movement, a revival without precedent in history.

Holiness Roots

America experienced several great revivals during the 18th and 19th centuries that prepared the way for the 20th-century outpouring of the Spirit. The revival that came to be called the Great Awakening "began in 1726 in the Raritan Valley of New Jersey in Dutch Reformed circles under the leadership of Theodore J. Frelinghuysen."[31] The Dutch Reformed churches were formal and spiritual vitality was low. Frelinghuysen, influenced by "Puritan emphases in

Holland, where he had been educated and ordained . . . sought to awaken his people to a deeper, more experiential knowledge of Christian faith."[32] After six years of effort, revival broke out in the churches under Frelinghuysen's care. Though many objected to the emotionalism that accompanied the revival, it attracted great attention, and its influence was felt in the Dutch Reformed churches for years.

The Dutch Reformed revival attracted the attention of a group of Presbyterians. One of them, Gilbert Tennent, became the central figure in a revival movement among Presbyterians. Two parties emerged in the Presbyterian church, eventually leading to a denominational split in 1745. The New York synod emphasized Puritan values and revival, while the Philadelphia synod insisted on strict adherence to the Westminster Confession.[33]

The Great Awakening spread to Congregational churches "when a remarkable revival swept the town of Northampton, Massachusetts, in 1734-35"[34] led by Congregational pastor Jonathan Edwards.

In 1739 the revival erupted again, spreading widely in New England. Congregational leaders were assisted in the work by Gilbert Tennent and George Whitefield, the latter then at the height of his youthful enthusiasm. Everywhere throngs hung on his words; faintings and outcries attended his sermons. As the awakening spread, hundreds were permanently changed. The spiritual condition of many communities was transformed.[35]

The Second Great Awakening "showed its first signs as early as 1792. By 1800, revival was in full tide. . . . The awakening was by no means limited to the Congregational churches, for Baptists flourished in an awakening atmosphere, and the Methodists, seeking a securer foothold in New England, freely used revivalistic practices."[36]

The revival soon spread into the Middle Atlantic states, the South, and west to the frontier. Camp meeting revivals began in Tennessee and Kentucky in 1800. These frontier revivals were "marked by emotional outcries and bodily manifestations."[37]

One of the most outstanding frontier revivals occurred at Cane Ridge in Logan County, Kentucky, in July 1800. Crowds of up to 25,000 people attended the camp meeting in which Baptists, Methodists, and Presbyterians participated.[38] Several ministers preached at the same time from preaching stands set up in various locations on the camp meeting grounds. At testimony time, as many as 300 laymen might be testifying at once.

A Methodist preacher, William Burke, reported, "Under the word of God, hundreds fell prostrate on the ground . . . and lay in agonies of distress, with a sinner occasionally jumping to his feet to give vent to 'shouts of triumph.'"[39]

"During this revival period, people shouted, exhorted with 'all possible ecstasy'; 'trances' were common, the 'mourners' bench was filled with penitent sinners, and often 'the floor was covered with the slain.'"[40]

Bernard A. Weisberger wrote:

Even if there had only been these things—the shouts, the wagons, the murmurous, plastic crowds, surging in the half darkness under the rain-beaten branches, Cane Ridge would have burned itself for life into the memories of men who were there. But stranger things were said to have happened; the power of the Lord was shown as it was when cloven tongues of fire sat upon the apostles. . . . At Cane Ridge, many men testified to the physical power of the Holy Spirit's baptism, which unstrung the knees and melted, with fervent heat, the hearts of the worshipers.[41]

The frontier revivals led to the "decline of 'infidelity,' the lifting of the moral level of the frontier, and the steady growth of Baptist, Methodist, and Presbyterian churches."[42]

Charles G. Finney, a giant of American revivalism, was a product of the Second Great Awakening. Converted in 1821, he began preaching and was ordained by the Presbyterian church.

Soon great revivals broke out under his fervent and intense preaching. He brought revival methods into an ordered pattern which became known as the "new measures." The measures—such as "unseasonable hours" for services, "protracted" meetings, the use of harsh and colloquial language, the specific naming of individuals in prayer and sermon, inquiry meetings, the "anxious bench"—were really not new, of course. It was the shaping of them into a system designed to produce results that was the novel feature. Despite the opposition of those who feared the emotionalism of frontier and "new measures" evangelism, Finney soon invaded the eastern cities. His tested methods soon came to be widely accepted and copied. The intensity and frequency of the revivals declined in the 1840's, but burst out again in new crescendo in 1857-1858, when a nationwide revival swept thousands in the churches. Daily prayer meetings, often at unusual hours, and lay leadership were features of this great peak in revival history.[43]

In the period following the Civil War,

the revival emphasis of American Protestantism was strongly continued. Lay evangelist Dwight L. Moody (1837-1899) was its most conspicuous exponent. Tireless organizer and aggressive pulpiteer, Moody was a powerful force in Protestant life. His revival methods were widely copied, and his missionary enthusiasm contributed significantly to the continued growth of the foreign missionary enterprise. But the intellectual atmosphere of the late nineteenth century was swift-changing, and many new views sharply challenged ideas cherished by conservative Protestants.[44]

Revival fires were burning low by the last quarter of the nineteenth century. Liberalism invaded many pulpits and theological schools. Complacency became the order of the day in the pews.

Discontent spread throughout the ranks of those who desired true revival. They fanned the dying embers of the revival fires with earnest prayer. But their efforts were mostly ignored by the major denominations or were rejected outright.

According to church historian Charles W. Conn,

the rift widened through a conspiracy of liberalistic influences. Everywhere, the Church became the scene of a struggle. Darwin's theory of evolution became one of the most devisive lines of combat. Sophistry replaced theology. The thought of Kant, Emerson, Newman, Voltaire, Schleiermacher, Carlyle, and a confusion of theologians, philosophers, and poets came to exert a greater influence on many a fashionable pulpit than did the Word of God. The Bible was largely forgotten. This hastened a deterioration of the evangelical life of the Church.[45]

This spiritual deterioration eventually led to the holiness separation. There is little evidence that the earliest holiness groups began with the intent of establishing new denominations. However, as the state of religion worsened,

> many earnest Christians who found the new liberalism unpalatable . . . withdrew from the churches and worshiped in small groups of kindred believers. A revival of modest proportions was born. Holiness groups—more than a score of them—gradually appeared on the American scene. . . . Holiness bands struggled to keep faith alive in the hearts of men. Inevitably, the groups of separatists, who no longer could go along with the older churches, became churches in their own right.[46]

One such group was led by a Baptist minister in the Unicoi Mountains of southeastern Tennessee, near the borders of North Carolina and Georgia. Protestantism was predominant in the region, but creeds and traditions had largely supplanted pristine worship.

> Ritual vied with faith; the church gained adherents to itself rather than to Christ; sin was condoned and embraced in spirit if not in word; denominational barriers developed a temper of steel; and rival denominations were denounced with much fiercer intent than was sin itself.[47]

A protracted meeting was held each year in every

church during the period after crops were laid by and before harvest. But the absence of true revivals troubled many sincere Christians.

In 1884, near the Cokercreek community in Monroe County, Tennessee, Richard G. Spurling, a Baptist licensed minister and pastor, combined prayer, Bible study, and a study of church history "in search of a way out of the morass of tradition, legalism, and ecclesiolatry."[48]

Spurling was often joined in prayer by his son, Richard G. Spurling, Jr., and another concerned Christian, John Plemons. For two years, they prayed earnestly and pled for reformation. Despite their praying, weeping, and pleading, revival did not come to their community.

After prayer and research, they concluded:

> In the sixteenth and seventeenth centuries, when the noble and illustrious reformers were throwing off and breaking out from under the galling yoke of Romanism, and launched what is commonly known as Protestantism, they failed to reform from creeds; they adopted the law of faith when they should have adopted the law of love; and third, they failed to reserve a right of way for the leadership of the Holy Ghost and conscience.[49]

In addition, they became aware that God's church exists only where His law and government are observed.

By the summer of 1886, the Cokercreek group realized that their reformation efforts were of no avail in their churches. They decided to hold a conference to determine a new course of action.

their churches. They decided to hold a conference to determine a new course of action.

On Thursday, August 19, 1886, the small group met at Barney Creek Meetinghouse, a crude log building about two miles from the Tennessee-North Carolina boundary.

The meeting opened with prayer for God's guidance. Richard G. Spurling "then arose and spoke passionately on the critical hour in which they lived, the need of spiritual reanimation and Christian unity, and the divine guidance that had brought them together. . . . Since reformation and holiness were resisted in the church, there must be a separation if there was to be genuine spiritual identity."[50]

Spurling then issued the following invitation to those present:

> As many Christians as are here present that are desirous to be free from all man-made creeds and traditions, and are willing to take the New Testament, or law of Christ, for your only rule of faith and practice; giving each other equal rights and privilege to read and interpret for yourselves as your conscience may dictate, and are willing to sit together as the Church of God to transact business as the same, come forward.[51]

Eight persons accepted the invitation. During the business session that followed, they chose Christian Union for their name, elected Spurling as their pastor, made provision for receiving new members into the group, and dedicated the body to the Lord. Spurling gave an unexplained second invitation before the meeting adjourned and a ninth member—Richard Spurling, Jr.—was added to the new church body.

Richard G. Spurling died soon after the formation of the Christian Union. Before his death he had ordained his son, R.G. Spurling, Jr., as pastor of the fledgling church on September 26, 1886.[52]

Preparing the Way

For the next 10 years the Christian Union made no noticeable progress although Spurling labored to revitalize worship in the churches. He traveled throughout the mountains, "extolling men everywhere to repent and manifest more of the nature of Christ. His exhortations were without immediate success, for they sounded on deaf ears and indifferent hearts."[53]

But Spurling faithfully prepared the way for the coming revival though he saw only meager results in his ministry. Spurling's preaching might have been more effective if he had preached holiness in a more positive light. According to Charles Conn, who interviewed a number of people who heard Spurling, his preaching "seems to have been mainly negative and denunciatory. . . . Nevertheless, he preached a form of holiness and sowed good seed that one day would bring forth abundantly. . . . Through the passion of his soul and the abundance of his labors, this valorous Christian kept aflame from 1886 to 1896 the spark that had been ignited by the Holy Spirit."[54]

In 1896 the holiness emphasis of the Christian Union began to bear fruit. Three laymen in the Cokercreek community were moved upon by the Spirit of God and began preaching sanctification.

William Martin, a Methodist, and Joe M. Tipton and Milton McNabb, both Baptists, traveled through the mountains preaching the same holiness message

Spurling had proclaimed for 10 years. But there was one difference: "Instead of viewing the subject in a negative way, they urged the people to seek a definite spiritual experience of sanctification which would make holiness not only possible but natural."[55] Since their message was not welcome in the established churches, the trio preached in private homes, under brush arbors, and outdoors to anyone who would listen.

At the same time, 14 miles away in Cherokee County, North Carolina, the Holy Spirit was preparing the way for revival in the mountains. A group of Baptists began to hold prayer meetings in their homes without sponsorship of any church. Since they had no regular preachers, they sang, testified, and prayed.

Martin, Tipton, and McNabb eventually began a revival at Camp Creek in Cherokee County. The men of the prayer meeting group arranged for the use of Shearer Schoolhouse, a one-room school located about a quarter-mile from the nearest house in the sparsely populated region.

The three evangelists preached "the necessity of Christian perfection—attainable through an experience of sanctification such as they had received."[56] Their understanding of holiness was strictly Wesleyan, but

> they did not preach the theology of sanctification as much as they exhorted from the Scriptures and related the wonderful experience they had received. What they lacked in preaching ability, theological training, and understanding, they made up in earnestness; all three were given much to prayer and fasting. Like Spurling, their exhortations were emotional and personal, and the results were unprecedented.[57]

The Christian Union moved their services to Camp Creek and the Tennessee and North Carolina groups became one, composed of believers from several communities. They had both prayed for the revival; together they would reap its benefits.

When the revival meeting closed, the holiness group began regular prayer meetings and Sunday school sessions. Though he often visited the Camp Creek congregation, Spurling continued to travel, preaching and promoting the new work. In his absence, Spurling chose William F. Bryant to lead the services. Under Bryant's able leadership, the revival continued.

Pentecost Comes to the Mountains

Twelve years had passed since Richard G. Spurling, Sr., had begun to voice his discontent with the religious status quo. Two years of prayer and exhortation had led to the formation of the Christian Union. Spurling's son had toiled tirelessly for another 10 years preparing the way for revival. Neither the Spurlings nor those who labored with them fully expected what happened next. They had prayed for a reformation; God sent a transformation.

For ten years the Spirit of God had been preparing the hearts of the people for something extraordinary. And now it happened. In seasons of fervent prayer, several of the members became so enraptured with the One to Whom they prayed that they were curiously moved by the Holy Spirit. . . . In ecstasy they spoke in languages unknown to those who heard the utterances. What had happened the simple, rustic Christians could not then understand, for within the memory of the oldest members of the Christian Union no such thing had been known. A total ignorance of church history prevented their knowledge of similar manifestations in other periods of awakening and revival. Soon others began to have similar ecstatic experiences, and, regardless of the place, time, or circumstances contingent to the experience, one manifestation was uniform in all: they spoke in tongues, or languages, unknown to those who listened in wonder and hope.[58]

Looking for an explanation for the strange manifestation, members of the Christian Union searched the Scriptures. They learned that the disciples had spoken in tongues when they were filled with the Holy Spirit on the Day of Pentecost (Acts 2:1-4). As they searched further, they found that the household of Cornelius had spoken in tongues (Acts 10:46) and that the believers in Ephesus also had spoken in tongues (Acts 19:6).

In each instance those exercised with the phenomenon were said to have received the Holy Ghost. So parallel were the biblical accounts to the experience of these people that recognition of what had happened became clear. A new outpouring of the Holy Ghost had occurred upon the earth.[59]

About 130 people received the Holy Spirit—which they called "the blessing"—in 1896.[60] However, the outside world knew nothing of what God was doing in these Southeastern mountains. Landlocked in their remote region, the people of the Christian Union had little contact with the outside world.

But if people outside the mountains knew nothing

of the new outpouring, neither were the mountain folk aware that people in other areas were receiving the Holy Spirit.

Similar experiences had occurred "among the Quakers; during the Methodist revival; to Edward Irving and his followers in 1830."[61] In *With Signs Following*, Stanley Frodsham wrote that the experience also was received by individuals in Rhode Island, 1875; Arkansas, 1879; Switzerland, 1879; Ohio, 1890; Minnesota, 1895; and South Dakota, 1896.[62] In January 1901, several people in Topeka, Kansas, received the Holy Spirit.[63] The Pentecostal revival spread to Texas in 1904-1905.[64]

The event that is recognized as the catalyst for the modern Pentecostal Movement began in Los Angeles, California, under the leadership of W.J. Seymour, a black Holiness preacher.

The Azusa Street revival, as it came to be known, broke out on April 9, 1906, when several people received the baptism in the Holy Spirit and spoke in tongues. Within a week, the group had rented an old building at 312 Azusa Street and started a mission.[65]

Unlike the 1896 outpouring in the Southeastern mountains, the revival at Azusa Street Mission was widely publicized. The *Los Angeles Times* sent a reporter to the mission the first week of the revival. Although his report was derogatory, it gave the Azusa Street revival a public forum. In addition, the mission published a newspaper, *The Apostolic Faith,* from September 1906 to May 1908.[66]

From Los Angeles, even then an international crossroads, the influence of the Azusa Street revival spread across America and the world as churches were established and people who were filled with the Spirit at Azusa Street carried the Pentecostal message to other countries.

The revival's influence can also be seen in its effect on churches. "Sometimes existing denominations were split, while others were totally transformed into Pentecostal vehicles. . . . But new groups were formed as well. . . . Indeed, nearly every Pentecostal denomination in the U.S. traces its roots in some way or other to the Apostolic Faith Mission at 312 Azusa Street."[67]

> Today the site of Azusa Street Mission is . . . unmarked except for the street sign. . . . Yet the phenomenal worldwide growth of the Pentecostal movement and its sister, charismatic renewal in the historic churches, suggests that the Azusa Street revival continues to bear much fruit.[68]

Outpourings of the Holy Spirit such as the one that came to the mountains of North Carolina in 1896 have melded into a worldwide movement that has profoundly affected 20th-century Christianity.

Unlike other great movements, the Pentecostal Movement was not led by any one man or group of men. Instead, this latter day outpouring of the Holy Spirit can be ascribed to nothing less than a sovereign move of God.

Jesus said, "The wind blows where it wishes, and you hear the sound of it, but cannot tell where it comes from and where it goes" (John 3:8, *NKJV*). On the Day of Pentecost, the Spirit came like a rushing mighty wind. The same wind of the Spirit is blowing across the world with a force that cannot be stopped. This mighty move of God transcends language and culture, race and religion. Political boundaries cannot keep the Spirit out. Hostile governments cannot forbid His work. Wherever the gospel is preached, the Spirit is falling upon hungry hearts.

And wherever the wind of the Spirit blows, people are being filled with the Holy Spirit as on the Day of Pentecost. At least 400 million people are Spirit-filled Christians today. Some estimates place the total number closer to a billion.

The prophet Joel foretold this day when he said, "And it shall come to pass afterward that I will pour out My Spirit on all flesh; your sons and your daughters shall prophesy, your old men shall dream dreams, your young men shall see visions: and also on My menservants and on My maidservants I will pour out My Spirit in those days" (2:28, 29, *NKJV*).

Joel's prophecy began to be fulfilled on the Day of Pentecost. When the people questioned what had happened that day, Peter said, "This is that which was spoken by the prophet Joel; and it shall come to pass in the last days, saith God, I will pour out of my Spirit upon all flesh: and your sons and your daughters shall prophesy, and your young men shall see visions, and your old men shall dream dreams: and on my servants and on my handmaidens I will pour out in those days of my Spirit; and they shall prophesy" (Acts 2:16-18). That prophecy is still being fulfilled today as God pours out His Spirit around the world.

This mighty move of God is bringing unprecedented revival. While religionists lament about a falling away, hungry hearts are abandoning the cold confines of religiosity and embracing the warmth of the Spirit-filled life.

Even in environments hostile to Christianity, the Holy Spirit is at work preparing a people for the coming of the Lord. "And the Spirit and the bride say, Come. And let him that heareth say, Come. And let him that is athirst come. And whosoever will, let him take the water of life freely" (Revelation 22:17).

Jesus said He would send the promise of the Father (Luke 24:49; Acts 1:4). The promise came on the Day of Pentecost and is yours today! "For the promise is unto you, and to your children, and to all that are afar off, even as many as the Lord our God shall call" (Acts 2:39).

Receive the Holy Spirit today and be *endued with power!*

Endnotes

[1] *The Interpreter's Dictionary of the Bible* (New York: Abingdon Press, 1962), IV, p. 672.

[2] G.B. Cutten, *Speaking With Tongues* (New Haven: Yale University Press, 1927), p. 113.

[3] Lefferts A. Loetscher, ed., *Twentieth Century Encyclopedia of Religious Knowledge* (Grand Rapids: Baker Book House, 1955), II, p. 1118.

[4] Philip Schaff, *History of the Apostolic Church,* Book I, Section 55, cited by Elmer C. Miller, *Pentecost*

Examined (Springfield, Missouri: Gospel Publishing House, 1936), p. 18.

⁵Madeleine S. Miller and J. Lane Miller, *Harper's Bible Dictionary* (New York: Harper and Brothers, 1952), p. 768.

⁶McCandlish Phillips, "And There Appeared to Them Tongues of Fire," *The Saturday Evening Post* (May 16, 1964), p. 32.

⁷"Tongues, Gift of" *Encyclopaedia Britannica*, 1958 ed.

⁸John E. Steinmueller and Kathryn Sullivan, *Catholic Biblical Encyclopedia* (New York: Joseph F. Wagner, 1956), p. 101.

⁹*Ibid.*, p. 258.

¹⁰F.L. Cross, "Glossolalia," *The Oxford Dictionary of the Christian Church* (London: Oxford University Press, 1958), p. 564.

¹¹R. Leonard Carroll, "Glossolalia: Apostles to the Reformation," *The Glossolalia Phenomenon*, Wade H. Horton, ed. (Cleveland, Tennessee: Pathway Press, 1966), pp. 76, 77.

¹²*Ibid.*, p. 77.

¹³*Ibid.*

¹⁴Irenaeus, "Against Heresies." *The Ante-Nicene Fathers*, American Series (Grand Rapids: Wm. B. Eerdmans Publishing Co., 1956), Vol. I, Book III, Chapter XVII, p. 444.

¹⁵*Ibid.*, Book V, Chapter VI, p. 531.

¹⁶Carroll, pp. 80, 81.

¹⁷Tertullian, "Tertullian Against Marcion," *The Ante-Nicene Fathers*, American Series (Grand Rapids: Wm.

B. Eerdmans Publishing Co., 1956), Vol. III, Book V, Chapter VIII, p. 447.

[18]Alban Butler, *The Lives of the Saints* (Baltimore: Murphy and Co., 1889), II, p. 218.

[19]Schaff, *History of the Apostolic Church*, III, p. 197.

[20]Origen, "Origen Against Celsus," *The Ante-Nicene Fathers* (New York: Charles Scribner's Sons, 1907), Vol. IV, Book VII, Chapter IX, p. 614.

[21]"Tongues, Gift of," *Encyclopaedia Britannica*, 1958, ed.

[22]Schaff, VI, p. 230.

[23]Butler, IV, p. 67.

[24]*Ibid.*, p. 73.

[25]*Ibid.*, III, p. 74.

[26]Miller, *Pentecost Examined*, p. 19.

[27]John Calvin, *Calvin's Commentaries: Corinthians*, Vol. I (Grand Rapids: Wm. B. Eerdmans Publishing Company, 1949), p. 437.

[28]David Smith, *The Life and Letters of St. Paul* (New York: Harper and Brothers, [n.d.], p. 229.

[29]*Ibid.*

[30]Taken from *The Works of John Wesley*, Vol. X, pp. 55, 56, cited by Vessie D. Hargrave, "Glossolalia: Reformation to the Twentieth Century," *The Glossolalia Phenomenon*, p. 103.

[31]Williston Walker, *A History of the Christian Church*, Third Edition (New York: Charles Scribner's Sons, 1970), p. 465.

[32]*Ibid.*

[33]*Ibid.*

[34] *Ibid.*

[35] *Ibid.*, p. 466.

[36] *Ibid.*, p. 507.

[37] *Ibid.*, p. 508.

[38] Hargrave, *The Glossolalia Phenomenon*, p. 105.

[39] Bernard A. Weisberger, *They Gathered at the River* (Boston: Little, Brown, and Company, 1958), p. 31.

[40] Hargrave, p. 106.

[41] Weisberger, pp. 33, 34.

[42] Walker, *A History of the Christian Church*, p. 508.

[43] *Ibid.*

[44] *Ibid.*, pp. 516, 517.

[45] Charles W. Conn, *Like A Mighty Army* (Cleveland, Tennessee: Pathway Press, 1973), p. xxiv.

[46] *Ibid.*, p. xxv.

[47] *Ibid.*, p. 4.

[48] *Ibid.*, p. 5.

[49] L. Howard Juillerat, *Book of Minutes* (Cleveland, Tennessee: Church of God Publishing House, 1922), pp. 7, 8.

[50] Conn, p. 7.

[51] Juillerat, p. 8.

[52] Conn, p. 13.

[53] *Ibid*, pp. 13, 14.

[54] *Ibid.*, pp. 15, 16.

[55] *Ibid.*, p. 17.

[56] *Ibid.*, p. 18.

[57] *Ibid.*, pp. 18, 19.

[58] *Ibid.*, p. 24.

[59] *Ibid.,* pp. 24, 25.

[60] Stanley M. Burgess and Gary B. McGee, eds., *Dictionary of Pentecostal and Charismatic Movements* (Grand Rapids: Zondervan Publishing House, 1988), p. 198.

[61] Conn, p. 24.

[62] Stanley H. Frodsham, *With Signs Following* (Springfield, Mo.: Gospel Publishing House, 1946), pp. 10–16.

[63] *Ibid.*, pp. 20, 21.

[64] *Ibid.*, pp. 27-29.

[65] Burgess and McGee, p. 32.

[66] *Ibid.*, pp. 32, 34.

[67] *Ibid.*, p. 35.

[68] *Ibid.*, p. 36.